How Do We Glorify God?

A SHORT GUIDE TO LIVING
A GOD-CENTRED LIFE

Daniel Klassen

HOW DO WE GLORIFY GOD?
Copyright © 2021 by Daniel Klassen

Print ISBN: 978-1-4866-2096-8
eBook ISBN: 978-1-4866-2097-5

Word Alive Press
119 De Baets Street, Winnipeg, MB R2J 3R9
www.wordalivepress.ca

WORD ALIVE
—P R E S S—

Cataloguing in Publication may be obtained through Library and Archives Canada

Daniel has written a wonderful work answering the question "How do we glorify God?" This guide on living a God-centered life is theologically robust, many times devotional in nature, and so practical on many levels. My heart was both challenged and encouraged to pursue glorifying God in all aspects of my life and I found myself, many times, worshiping God as I read these pages. Make sure to grab a pen and notepad as you work your way through the lofty concepts and truths that Daniel wonderfully explains.

—Steve Janz
Executive Director
Millar College of the Bible, Sunnybrae Campus
Tappen, BC

Daniel does a great job of bringing the historical events of the Reformation together with Biblical truth and spelling out in layman's terms, both the necessity and practicality of life to the glory of God. It serves as a good reminder for me to stay focused on Christ and the glory of God.

—Merlis Wiebe
Lay Pastor
Bergthaler Mennonite Church
Saskatchewan, SK

It seems to me that the "gos*pill*" is fashionable these days. The "gos*pill*" is a placebo, a remedy for all that ails us. It's a spiritual pill that we take in Jesus name, that promises to fix everything that's broken. The "Gospel" is different. The gospel is the good news of Jesus Christ. It's good news that Christ loves us, chooses us, pursues us, convicts us, forgives us, in order to heal us. The gospel changes us from the inside out. In Daniel's most recent book "How Do We Glorify God," he moves the reader from transformation to implementation. Daniel challenges us to live what we believe. Daniel believes with passion that the Gospel isn't mere proclamation. No, it's demonstration. The gospel must affect our character, thinking, practice, and ultimately, our submission to Jesus. What makes this book worthwhile to read? Daniel lives what he writes.

—Greg Pearson
Pastor
First Baptist Victoria
Victoria, BC

For Delten & Luke

Iron sharpens iron, and one man sharpens another.

—Proverbs 27:17

Contents

Acknowledgements

No book is written alone, and this one is no exception. This book is a long time coming, longer than all my other writings. Before I ever started writing, it was the first idea I had for a book, but it has taken until now to put it together. During the early stages of writing my initial thoughts, both Greg Pearson and David Hutchinson helped me think better about the various subjects by pointing out where I could be more precise in my writing. They have my gratitude.

Many thanks to Word Alive Press for their encouragement and excitement in my project. When I submitted my manuscript to the publishing contest, I wasn't entirely confident in my project. However, making it onto the non-fiction shortlist was a major boost for me to go ahead and get it published.

I am thankful for my church for being a place where I am challenged, encouraged, and helped along in becoming more Christ-like, one conducive to glorifying God in every part of life. These thanks are for my parents, who brought me to church from the moment I was born, making sure I attended Sunday School and youth group to increase my understanding of Scripture and love for God while making the faith my own. It is also for my pastors who faithfully preach God's Word (intent on glorifying God), and take time to personally invest in my life to help me glorify God better.

I am also grateful to the men and women who have gone before me, who taught and displayed a God-centred life. Most of them are not alive to hear my gratitude. Nevertheless, they still inspire through the writings they left behind. These resources are invaluable to me as a Christian, husband, thinker, teacher, and writer.

I am most thankful for my wife Annette, my ardent supporter and greatest encouragement in writing. She willingly listens to me ramble on about ideas and different ways to express those ideas, and when I lack motivation for writing, she makes sure I get some words on the page. More importantly, she inspires me to better live to the glory of God.

Finally, as in all things, thanks be to God.

Introduction

Between the years 1643 and 1653, the Westminster Divines[1] came together to produce a standard of church government, teaching, and worship for the Church of England. Their efforts produced one of the most influential confessions of faith and most memorized catechisms, which would later be adopted by the Church of Scotland, certain Baptists and Congregationalists in England, and the majority of American Protestant denominations. Their first question and answer are perhaps the most memorable and often recited of all catechism answers.

> **Question:** What is the chief end of man?
> **Answer:** Man's chief end is to glorify God and enjoy Him forever.

Why, do you think, did they begin with this question? Why not start with something more important, like the nature of God or the key elements of the gospel? I think it is because the answer summarizes everything Scripture says concerning

---

1 A Divine was a student of theology, called a "Divine" because of their understanding and knowledge of Scripture.

man's relation to God and others. Every subsequent question and answer tied into it. To be created for God means we are created to glorify God *and* find our highest enjoyment in Him. We are not made for anything except this end. According to the Westminster Divines, the Christian life is not dull nor miserable servitude, but a life of joy, a happy life, and it is that way because it is a life of glorifying God.

Some might object to their answer because it is too simple for a problem we all face, while others might object because it sounds too pious and religious. They might accuse the Divines of gathering in an ivory tower echo chamber, disconnected from the common people. They might say these men were too heavenly minded to be of any earthly good. All these objections, however, don't hold much weight. The assembly was formed amid political revolutions[2] and religious pluralism, and the men who gathered were not untouched by the surrounding events. Threats from political and religious powers loomed overhead as they discussed and debated theological points. Some of the Divines had political motivations; others had more sincere reasons for assembling. As for outside influences, they cited philosophers such as Aristotle, early Church fathers such as Tertullian, Ambrose, Augustine, and Cyprian, and Reformers such as Luther, Calvin, Beza, and Bucer. Many of the participants were simple clergymen, trained in theology and well-acquainted with the trenches of their local congregations. They understood the "real life" of suffering, pain, fear, hope, joy, sorrow, and were active in pastoring, counselling, and caring for their people. Some of the men in attendance were later forcefully removed from their pulpits by the government in The Great Ejection of 1662. These

---

2   This was during the time of the English Civil Wars (1642-1651). The Westminster Assembly formed in part because of the religious aspect of the civil wars, and in part because they saw the need to reform the church again.

Divines were Puritans, set on reforming England, from the simple plowboy to the king and queen, for the glory of God.

One such Puritan was Thomas Watson (c. 1620-1686). Although he was not part of the assembly, he advocated for the widespread use of the Westminster Standards, and during his ministry, he preached a series on the Shorter Catechism to explain each answer from Scripture. These sermons were later published after his death as *A Body of Divinity*. Watson's book covers the basic Christian understanding of God's character and attributes, man's fall into sin, God's covenant with man, God's redemption of man, and death and the resurrection. Watson emphasized what the Divines had realized in their first question of the catechism, that before a Christian rightly understands the whole of Scripture, they must understand the glory of God.

I remember hearing about a student who asked his seminary professor if the Westminster Standards were perfect. The professor replied, "No, they aren't perfect. But, they understand the Bible a whole lot better than you, and your understanding of the Bible would benefit from reading them."

Both the Divines and Watson did not pull their theology from out of thin air. They reached the conclusion that God's glory underlines our understanding of Scripture by their faithful commitment to speak precisely about Scripture, and in doing so, only spoke as far as God's Word allowed.

We find the Puritan precedent in the Old Testament, in that every instance where people come into the presence of God, their experience of God always has to do with His glory. In Moses's story, God refers to His presence as "glory," and because His glory was so great, He had to hide Moses behind a rock, only able to show His back.[3] Isaiah also saw God's glory,[4] which

---

3   Exodus 33:17-23
4   Isaiah 6:1-7

he described as "the train of his robe," and this robe "filled the temple." In the presence of God, Isaiah found no room for anything other than God's glory. The New Testament corresponds with these Old Testament examples in the story of Jesus. At His birth, the angels were surrounded by God's glory as they appeared to the lowly shepherds, and their praise echoed Isaiah's story: "Glory to God in the highest, and on earth peace among those with whom he is pleased!"[5] The apostle John explains this event when he wrote, "And the Word became flesh and dwelt among us, and we have seen his glory, glory as of the only Son from the Father, full of grace and truth."[6] It is, therefore, no surprise the Divines began with the glory of God because the gospel is a story of glory. It is the glory of God come to us to save us from our failure to glorify Him, and it comes to turn our lives into lives that glorify Him.

It is essential to keep the glory of God at the forefront of our gospel because it keeps us from many errors. Among those Christians face, moralism and liberalism rise to the top in popularity. They begin as subtle mistakes that enter the doors of many churches undetected. Soon they begin to grow, and can subvert the entire gospel. Moralism turns the gospel from a work which God has done for us into a work which we do for God, so it takes the Christian's eyes off the glory of God, not only in salvation but in every aspect of life. On the other hand, liberalism appears to promote free grace, but its underlining goal is to justify pet sins. Sin, however, never stays a pet. It morphs into something much greater and more powerful than any person can handle. But no matter its size, the problem of sin is at its root that it falls short of the glory of God.[7] It denies the author-

---

5   Luke 2:14
6   John 1:14
7   Romans 3:23

ity of God's Word, rejecting every instruction of God to live life the way He intended.

The Westminster Divines purposely attached the enjoyment of God to the glorification of God, not as a separate part of man's chief end, but closely connected because they understood that to live life the way God intends is the only way to live a satisfying life. Christ taught to believe in Him is to "have life and have it abundantly."[8] Paul explains it this way, "We have peace with God through our Lord Jesus Christ."[9] In other words, Jesus satisfies our deepest longings if we live for Him. This reality leaves us with only one conclusion: our goal in life—in thinking, believing, feeling, loving, doing—must revolve around one question: what does it mean to glorify God?

In this short book, we will follow Thomas Watson as he unpacks the first question and answer of the Shorter Catechism, particularly to answer the question of what glorifying God means in a practical sense.

---

8   John 10:10
9   Romans 5:1b

CHAPTER ONE

Living to Glorify God

WHAT IS THE MEANING AND PURPOSE OF LIFE?

This is perhaps the fundamental question of life, and it seems we feel it in our innermost parts. We do not have to observe the people around us for long to see how central a role purpose plays in life. Humanity is driven by the need for purpose—and meaningful purpose at that—so the goal of life is to find where both meaning and purpose meet. Initially, this need was never one we had to work to find because man was not separated from God before sin. The quest for purpose was fulfilled within Adam the day God created him, but such is not the case now that sin is part of our nature. We are bereft of God, leaving our need for purpose unanswered, leaving us to search for it in all sorts of wrong places.

To answer the question with something as simple as glorifying God, as the Westminster Divines did, challenges our modern solutions. The meaningful purpose concocted in our modern time can be summarized by an old Taoist proverb: "The journey is the reward." Robert Louis Stevenson, who famously captured the struggle of good and evil in *The Strange Case of Dr. Jekyll and Mr. Hyde*, also agreed with the Taoists when he wrote "To travel hopefully is a better thing than to arrive."[10] For many today, the journey itself is the purpose. Maybe the reason they journey with no intention of finding a destination is they are frightened by an unknown place, or maybe every one they've ever arrived at tremendously disappointed them. Nevertheless, they are resolved to always travel. It could also be they are enticed by a journey without demands, a journey where they are free to do whatever they want. Once a demand is made, the journey to nowhere in particular ends because a demand creates and requires direction. But regardless of the reason, a journey without a destination is not a journey, it is the act of being lost in meaninglessness. The definite answer and conclusive destination of glorifying God is the best antidote for those lost in an empty journey.

There are also many who opt for destinations "under the sun"[11] to make their journey purposeful, but that, too, is problematic because those kinds of journeys only last a season. They find immediate purpose, but because the purpose has no eternal meaning for life, it soon fades.

It turns out the quest for purpose is not as much about purpose as it is about meaning. We all face the fact we will die, and as long as we face that fact, we will ask what the meaning of life is for us. That question underlines our quest for purpose. If the destination has no ultimate meaning, why set off on a journey for it? We need a purpose for our journey, and we need it to be meaningful. However, if we live "under the sun", what we think is meaningful in this life is subjective up to the point of death. Say for instance I consider a thing meaningful "under the sun" and you do not; that is subjective preference and it matters little. My meaningful purpose matters little to you because you have to find your own.

---

10   Robert Louis Stevenson. *Virginibus Puerisque* (London, UK: C. Kegan Paul & Co., 1881), 190.

11   Solomon's description of life without regard for God, found in Ecclesiastes.

However, it matters a great deal in the face of death. What if my meaningful purpose means nothing when I die, or yours when you die? Death without meaning is a horrible existence. It is nihilistic. If death has no meaning, the life which is brought to an end by death loses its meaning. To find meaning in life, it must be a meaning which both includes and transcends death.

SINGING FOR MEANINGFUL PURPOSE

There was a time in my teen years when I distinctly understood my voice was in the process of maturing rapidly, and because it was in such a fluctuating state, I questioned the necessity of singing. Some people, I realized, found it enjoyable to sing, but in my mind, it was because they were good at it. I could barely focus through the duration of a congregational hymn in church, especially when the congregation sang five stanzas and a lengthy refrain. It was torturous. When I found somewhat of a decent singing voice in my late teens that wouldn't draw attention for being too far out of tune, I was still bored when singing. Most of my issue was in my failure to understand the purpose of singing. Only when I was swept up in the purpose of singing did I find enjoyment in the song. It had nothing to do with my voice or the number of stanzas to sing, but everything to do with my devotion to God. Singing, I found, is what Christians do when the words and doctrines are too wonderful to speak; where we have no other recourse but to sing.

That is what happened to Paul at the end of Romans 11. Paul's epistle to the Romans is a logical and thorough work on how the gospel saves both Jew and Gentile alike. He starts with the shared sinfulness of humanity, then moves to the kind of faith that saves, then to how it saves completely, and then to the eternal promise of the gospel. As a result, Paul cannot help but break out into praise for the glorious work of God in saving sinners.

> Oh, the depth of the riches and wisdom and knowledge of God! How unsearchable are his judgments and how inscrutable his ways! For who has known the mind of the Lord, or who has been his counselor? Or who has given a gift to him that he might be repaid? For from him and through him and to him are all things. To him be glory forever. Amen.[12]

Perhaps Paul's words of praise are surprising to many modern believers brought up on a steady diet of contemporary Christian music. Modern Christian music isn't void of theology, but it is often watered down. Paul, however, is profoundly theological in his praises. He aims straight for God's glory without flinching. There is no time for the theology of modern liberalism, which makes God out to be a cosmic Santa Claus, a God without severity and judgement, and only filled with the resemblance of human love. Paul portrays God as God has pleased to reveal Himself in His Word, and God has pleased to reveal Himself as a self-sufficient God:

> For who has known the mind of the Lord, or who has been his counselor? Or who has given a gift to him that he might be repaid?

That is the essence of God, without which He would not be God.

Paul's goal in praising God's self-sufficiency and sovereignty is not to spark questions over the existence of evil (although

---

they are included), but to express the otherness of God. It is the only way Paul can express his deepest feelings in his relation to God, and as he does, he cannot help but intertwine God's glory with life's most meaningful purpose. All things are from God, sustained by God, and exist for God, so the purpose of all things is to glorify God. The point Paul makes is God's glory is *itself* meaningful purpose because it transcends this life.

FOUNDATIONS FOR GLORIFYING GOD

Before Thomas Watson began illustrating the practical ways we glorify God, he set a foundation of four principles that summarize every piece of practical advice he, or anyone else for that matter, could give. To begin with principles helps us to apply practical advice more efficiently; if you cannot remember the practical, you can still rely on the principle. Principles help build the character necessary for consistent application. Watson's four principles for glorifying God, which he calls "pillars," are appreciation, adoration, affection, and subjection.

The first pillar is appreciation, or esteem. It is the essence of the first three commandments given to Moses on Mount Sinai: "You shall have no other gods before Me", "You shall not make for yourself an idol" and "You shall not take the name of the Lord your God in vain."[13] It is also the first petition Jesus teaches us to pray: "Hallowed be Your name."[14] To esteem God is to set God as the highest in our thinking. It is to admire Him, to stand in awe of Him, to be captivated by His beauty and the beauty He created, to treasure His promises found in His gospel, to allow the scriptural description of God to stand over against our own wishes and imaginations. Setting God in such a place

13   Exodus 20:3-7
14   Matthew 6:9; Luke 11:2

of honour will promote our spiritual wellbeing. As Augustine (A.D. 354-430) once wrote, "To think the best of God is the truest foundation of piety."[15]

The second pillar of Watson's foundation is adoration, or worship. Our worship reveals what we most esteem. Therefore, it is when we have set God in the highest place of honour that we will properly worship Him. To worship God is to ascribe to Him what is due to His name. The psalmist writes, "Ascribe to the Lord the glory due His name; Worship the Lord in the splendor of holiness."[16] This does not mean we give to God more glory than He already possesses, but that we acknowledge the glory He already has. Isaiah saw God "with the train of His robe filling the temple,"[17] meaning God's glory was full; it could not sustain addition in Isaiah's day, and it cannot in our day, and will not for every generation to come.

The overarching point in Watson's second pillar is God is only glorified by our worship if our worship is pleasing to Him. He is not pleased when we attempt to add glory to His name. Just as in the meticulous and precise building of the tabernacle, or the appointed form of worship for the children of Israel, so is the border of our worship set by God. We cannot add, nor leave out anything in the pattern of worship described for us in His Word. Anything other than spiritual and truthful worship[18] amounts to the strange fire presented to God by the sons of Aaron.[19]

Affection, or love, for God is the third pillar of glorifying Him, and it is another facet in our esteem of God. If we do not esteem God properly, we will not love Him with true love. We

---

15   Augustine. *Augustine: Earlier Writings* (Philadelphia, PA: The Westminster Press, 1953), 115.

16   Psalm 29:2

17   Isaiah 6:1

18   John 4:23

19   Leviticus 10:1

do not love God with the self-love of this world, in that a person will only love another when they do something good to them. For instance, if we love God because He has blessed us, it reveals our true delight is in God's blessings rather than God Himself. True love for God, as Thomas Watson describes, is when "the heart is set upon God—as a man's heart is set upon his treasure."[20] It is to delight in God as He is and for who He is. We could just as well say it is to have God seated upon the throne of our hearts. Therefore, to love God in the way that glorifies Him, God is set in the highest place of honour, *and we delight in it*.

If the previous three pillars are established in our character, thinking, and practice, the fourth pillar of subjection is the obvious conclusion. If God takes preeminence in your life, you must submit to Him; you must dedicate yourself to His service. Jesus connects these together when He states, "If you love Me, you will keep My commandments."[21] In essence, the result of love, esteem, and adoration is obedience. When we esteem, adore, and delight in God, we naturally submit to His will above our will. We do not begin with obedience because it cannot cause a proper view of God to be formed in us, nor can it cause a proper love to abide within. Obedience flows from the fountain of esteem and adoration. It serves as the test of glorifying God because it is the most visible pillar of glorifying God.

AIMING AT GOD'S GLORY

From Thomas Watson's four pillars, the first practical step to glorifying God is to make His glory the sole aim in life. We must take this step before we attempt any further practical actions.

---

20   Thomas Watson, *A Body of Divinity* (Carlisle, PA: Banner of Truth Trust, 2015), 8.
21   John 14:15

What it means to make God's glory our sole aim in life is not only to advance His glory in this world but to aim at it with everything we do. Our aim must never be for our own glory, since to aim for our glory is pride and vainglory—it is sin. Watson describes this distinction when commenting on Jesus' words "When you give alms, do not sound a trumpet"[22]:

> A stranger would ask, 'What means the noise of this trumpet?' It was answered, 'They are going to give to the poor.' And so they did not give alms—but sell them for honor and applause, that they might have glory of men. The breath of men was the wind which blew the sails of their charity![23]

Selling alms for glory is the essence of sin because it is the preference of self-glory above everything else. Sin is not only found in the action but also in the motivation to act. To aim solely at the glory of God is to prefer it over everything else; over reputation, wealth and possessions, and relations. Everything must submit to the glory of God and be carried out for the glory of God. This requires the committed aim Jesus speaks about when He says that if a man cannot forsake their own family members for Him, they are unworthy of Him.[24]

In The Lord's Prayer,[25] Jesus teaches us the form of God-glorifying prayer. In the first three petitions ("Hallowed be your name;" "Your kingdom come;" "Your will be done") He teaches our primary aim in prayer and life must be for the glory of God. The first petition is for the hallowing of God's name, which is an act our modern English vocabulary cannot describe with a single word. We are left with the antiquated

---

22   Matthew 6:2
23   Thomas Watson, *A Body of Divinity* (Carlisle, PA: Banner of Truth Trust, 2015), 10.
24   Matthew 10:37
25   Matthew 6:9-14

word, "hallowed," which is a combination of "make holy" and "glorify". It consists of asking God to display His holiness and glory, and aligning ourselves with that mission—a mission that combines esteem, adoration, and worship into one fluid motion. The second and third petitions are similar. They are for God's kingdom and will to rule on this earth in the hearts of people. Essentially, these describe in practical terms what it looks like to aim for God's glory.

Prioritizing God's glory in all of life is opposed to our nature. Only by faith do we desire the will of God over and against our will. To live this out, we put on the mind of Christ, praying as he did in the garden, "not my will, but yours be done."[26] He was content to endure even the worst suffering if God would be glorified through it. For us, this means we place all the things we want most in life at the feet of God. When we do that, we will share the same desire as Watson: "Let my candle go out, if the Son of Righteousness may but shine."[27] Or, as Paul writes,

> Some indeed preach Christ from envy and rivalry, but others from good will. The latter do it out of love, knowing that I am put here for the defense of the gospel. The former proclaim Christ out of selfish ambition, not sincerely but thinking to afflict me in my imprisonment. What then? Only that in every way, whether in pretense or in truth, Christ is proclaimed, and in that I rejoice.[28]

Paul's desire was to let Christ, "the Son of Righteousness," shine, even if his candle of influence and popularity went out. Sure, the reason these people preached Christ was because they

---

26   Luke 22:42
27   Thomas Watson, *A Body of Divinity* (Carlisle, PA: Banner of Truth Trust, 2015), 11.
28   Philippians 1:15-18

saw the popularity of Paul and wished for the same. But though these men preached for their own glory, their message had the possibility of bringing glory to God, and that was just fine with Paul—their motives and actions were between them and God. Paul's commitment to the glory of God was such that if others outshone him in preaching, he would still rejoice.

To glorify God, we must be content to let our light go out so Christ's light might shine more clearly through us. This shift from self-glory to God's glory transforms our entire lives, even down to our daily routines. We will not aim for our own glory, or for the glory of man, but for a glory outside the material world. The places we work will notice how effective we become, because we are no longer working for ourselves but to serve others for God's glory. We will be most grateful in eating and drinking, because our awareness of God's provision is heightened when we aim at His glory. In every aspect of life— marriage, parenting, social interactions, etc.—our approach is enhanced because our aim is set on the One who needs nothing, but "gives to all mankind life and breath and everything."[29]

Make the glory of God your chief aim in life. Get a robust theology to inform your worship. Set God in the highest place of honour. Worship Him for who He is, not what you want Him to be. Submit to His will and obey Him, for in doing so, you display your love for Him. Then, aim for His glory in all you do, and you will find meaningful purpose and eternal joy.

---

29   Acts 17:25

CHAPTER TWO

The Glory of God in Salvation

WE GLORIFY GOD BY BELIEVING IN HIM. THIS SOUNDS LIKE A SIMPLE proposition, a plain command for us to follow, but it isn't. Part of the difficulty is that belief in God is a multiplication of doctrines Christians hold all at once. The other part is growing in our understanding of each doctrine. Many Christians who grow in their knowledge of God, and begin to understand His greatness, often resort to the comforts of their childhood understanding of Him and concern themselves with more practical matters. The greatness and otherness of God creates many complexities and difficulties not only because it forces Christians to rethink their understanding of many other topics but because it takes them to the edge of knowledge, where their curiosity wishes to know God beyond what has been revealed. Some indulge their curiosities to their demise. For the majority, however, they would rather not be bothered. Nevertheless, the Christian is expected to increase their knowledge of God continually.

What does it mean to increase in knowledge, and how is it done in a way that doesn't go beyond the boundaries of revelation?

Prying into the secret things of God, such as His divine will and eternal attributes, doesn't glorify God. It indicates a distrust in God's ability to reveal enough about His character and nature necessary to live a godly life. To stop within the bounds of revelation as we grow in knowledge, we must turn to a classical understanding of God. This means we turn to His revealed nature and attributes, and we piece them together, not as separate parts, but as the whole character and nature of God. Classical theism begins with divine simplicity[30] as the summary of God's nature, and it consists of God being immutable (changeless), impassible (unaffected by anything in the created order), and eternal (outside of time and space). With this framework, we are well-equipped to understand God's power, wisdom, holiness, sovereignty, righteousness, goodness, and love.[31] Growth in understanding God's character and nature calms our curiosity and turns our prying into appreciation, adoration, affection, and subjection.

The greater problem, however, in believing in God is that it is unnatural for our sinful nature. To assume belief in God comes as naturally as a child learning to walk is similar to assuming that since the child has learned to walk, it must be able to learn to fly. Likewise, a person can be taught in the Bible and come to believe there is a God, but that is quite different than that same person being taught and believing *in* God. For some, to believe there is a God means having a moralistic worldview where God is just a lawgiver and judge; or a therapeutic worldview where God exists solely for their benefit; or a deistic worldview where God is a distant power, uninvolved in their lives.[32] Others may go to the extent of believing God is the sovereign

---

30   Divine simplicity can also be understood as God's perfection, in that He is not made of created parts but exists in and of Himself.

31   Edward Feser, "Classical theism," EdwardFeser.Blogspot.com, September 30, 2010, http://edwardfeser.blogspot.com/2010/09/classical-theism.html, accessed December 2020.

32   Moralistic therapeutic deism is a term coined by sociologist Christian Smith in his book, *Soul Searching,* to describe the religion of postmodern teenagers and young adults.

creator of the universe intricately involved in our lives, but because it is nothing more than a general belief, they will inevitably believe the only way to appease God is by their good works. Since they are generally concerned with God, they are generally concerned with morals—which is a good thing for society—but they all still lack the most important part: true faith.

THE GIFT OF FAITH

Faith is not something we are born with, nor is it something we learn; it is given to us by God. On the contrary, many Christians assume everyone inherently has faith. The faith they assume unbelievers have is not faith but common trust. It is as one putting their "faith" in the taxi driver or airline pilot to transport them to their destination without any difficulties. But that is simply optimistic hope or mathematical probability; since the large majority of people using these means of transportation make it to their destination safely, there is a good chance no accident will occur when they use that mode of transportation. True faith, however, is given to us by God through Scripture for the purpose of trusting fully in Christ. As Paul writes, "So faith comes from hearing, and hearing through the word of Christ."[33]

God is glorified by faith because He is the one who gives it. He is glorified by any act of faith which follows because it points to Him as the giver, not the one who uses it. For example, when someone is given a gift which greatly increases their abilities, it would be foolish to boast in their abilities. Rather they will boast in the one who gave the increase every time they use that ability. We find this idea in Jesus' parable of the talents.[34] It is a story of a master who gives each his servants a specific amount

33   Romans 10:17
34   Matthew 25:14-30

of money to steward while he is away. Any investments the three servants made was only possible because the master gave them money. If he had not given the talents, they wouldn't have had the capacity to invest. That meant any return they received which increased their overall amount glorified the master, not themselves. They were responsible for keeping, stewarding, and investing, but both the gifting of the money and the return on the investment were not of them.

Paul later explains the spiritual meaning of this parable to the Ephesians.

> For by grace you have been saved through faith. And this is not your own doing; it is the gift of God, not a result of works, so that no one may boast. For we are his workmanship, created in Christ Jesus for good works, which God prepared beforehand, that we should walk in them.[35]

The key phrase in this short passage is clearly, "so that no one may boast," because the whole passage rests on it. Why does God save? So that no one may boast! Why does nothing of salvation originate in us? So that no one may boast! Why is it not our decision or action that saves us? So that no one may boast! Paul's following sentence also rests on it: "we… are created in Christ Jesus for good works which God prepared beforehand, that we should walk in them." Even the good works we do are completely reliant on the grace and gifting from God.

The common reason why Christians might erroneously disregard this teaching is they believe in merited blessings. They are certain that in order to be blessed in an unbiased manner, they must be blessed because they deserved it. The acts which are to be blessed must originate solely within themselves and

---

35   Ephesians 2:8-10

not from God, so they believe God cannot give the blessings of faith and salvation without some form of their merit. The trouble with this trajectory is it does not take much effort to sustain this error. When the Bible clearly states the righteous are blessed, and the unrighteous are cursed, they liberally assume how these people became righteous; that one day they decided to be righteous to escape the curse of the unrighteous. The whole of Scripture, however, does not agree with their assumption. Scripture does not place humanity in a neutral state, unbiased in their choice between righteousness and unrighteousness, but places humanity in the realm of the unrighteous, incredibly biased towards their realm.

> "None is righteous, no, not one;
>> no one understands;
>> no one seeks for God.
> All have turned aside; together they have become worthless;
>> no one does good,
>> not even one." [36]

Humanity inherited its sinful nature from Adam, the federal head of all people. This means all people live under the curse of God for their inherited unrighteousness. Along with this, the Bible warns those who try to obtain righteousness by their own efforts that they continue in unrighteousness. "All our righteous deeds are like a filthy garment," says Isaiah.[37] However, it is exactly at this point—when we were ungodly sinners, fully deserving the curse—that Christ died for us.[38] We had no hope

---

36   Romans 3:10-12
37   Isaiah 64:6
38   Romans 5:8

of righteousness apart from God acting to obtain righteousness for us.

The only conclusion we are left with is God does not bless us on the basis of merit, but blesses the work of his grace and mercy. More particularly, God gives faith according to His gracious will, not according to our merit.

COMING TO GOD THROUGH CHRIST

When the Bible tells us God gives faith according to His grace, a particularly special faith is implied. It is not universal faith, nor is it the same kind of "faith" found in the many religions in the world. The reason this faith is special is its object is Christ.

The apostle John desired his readers to understand the importance of belief in Christ, so he made sure to emphasize Jesus' teachings about belief in God through the Son. In John's gospel, the theme of belief in the context of unity between the Son and the Father is picked up in the opening verses and carried out through to the end. John's theme is simple: the key of faith is Christ, and without Him, no one will arrive at knowing God the Father.

In John's account of the Last Supper,[39] he gives us a peek into the conversation around the table. Over the course of the evening, the topic of conversation turned to the coming event of Jesus' death (John 14). Jesus reassured His disciples not to be troubled: "Believe in God; believe also in me."[40] Why? Because He was going to His Father to prepare a place for them; because He would come again to take them to where He was. This caused more questions than it gave answers. "Thomas said to him, Lord, we do not know where you are going. How can we

---

39   John 13-17
40   John 14:1

know the way?"[41] Jesus' response profoundly connected Himself to the Father.

> "I am the way, and the truth, and the life. No one comes to the Father except through me. If you had known me, you would have known my Father also. From now on you do know him and have seen him."[42]

In the context of salvation, Jesus is teaching that no one can truly come to the Father, that is, restore their relationship with God, unless they come through faith in His death and resurrection. If we want nothing to do with Christ, we will have nothing to do with the Father, no matter how convinced we are that our good works please Him. On the other hand, if we want nothing to do with the Father, we have nothing to do with Christ, no matter how sincerely we follow in His footsteps.

Philip needed more. He asked, "Lord, show us the Father, and it is enough for us."[43] Jesus responded the same way as when He defended Himself against the Pharisees not long before. His answer again affirms if we do not come to the Father through Him, we do not come to the Father nor glorify God in our faith.

> Jesus said to him, "Have I been with you so long, and you still do not know me, Philip? Whoever has seen me has seen the Father. How can you say, 'Show us the Father'? Do you not believe that I am in the Father and the Father is in me? The words that I say to you I do not speak on my own authority, but the Father who dwells in me does his works.

---

41   John 14:5
42   John 14:6-7
43   John 14:8

Believe me that I am in the Father and the Father is in me,
or else believe on account of the works themselves."[44]

According to Jesus, the importance of having the right
kind of faith is overwhelming. It is the glue holding together every way in which we glorify God in our salvation and in
every aspect of the Christian life. Christ must be the object of
our faith if we are to know the Father and thereby glorify Him.
Possessing the right kind of faith is then paramount to living a
life that glorifies God. As Paul states, "For whatever does not
proceed from faith is sin."[45]

THE WORK OF FAITH

God is not only glorified by being the gracious giver of faith,
but also by the fruit of faith produced in us. Faith is the act of
completely depending on God by believing the finished work of
Christ is powerful enough to bring complete salvation, and by
taking Him at His Word always. Therefore, faith takes our eyes
off ourselves and places them on Christ. Faith truly changes our
lives. It causes us to see God as good and His promises as true, and
by faith we come to trust the promises of God, which become
our possession. Faith honours God because it believes God is who
He says He is, all the while seeing ourselves as in desperate need
of him.

Unbelief, on the other hand, dishonours God because it
makes God be a liar. The apostle John particularly points out the
unbeliever deals directly with God although they want nothing to
do with Him. John writes, "Whoever believes in the Son of God
has the testimony in himself. Whoever does not believe God has

---

44   John 14:9-11
45   Romans 14:23b

made him a liar, because he has not believed in the testimony that God has borne concerning his Son."[46] The unbeliever has substantial evidence to believe, but turns their face away; bountiful gifts of mercy await, but they trust their own wisdom and strength.

The one who believes flees to God to find refuge in His mercy and grace. He makes himself a prisoner to the promises, binding himself to them and trusting God with everything he has. Thomas Watson captures it poetically, "Faith knows there are no impossibilities with God, and will trust him, where it cannot trace him."[47] Those who have faith are walking miracles. The thing all the wisdom and knowledge in the world could not do is done in the heart by faith. Faith makes an enemy into a child, a proud man into a humble man, the unrighteous into the righteous, and transforms a life dishonouring to God into a life glorifying Him.

THE PRAISE OF HIS GLORY

The highest and purest act of religion is praising God. No other Christian act of worship encompasses as much as praise since it transcends all stages, circumstances, and areas of life. Praise concludes all doctrine, and because praise glorifies God, it must consume the believer.

God deserves praise simply because there is no one greater to praise. No one rises above God, nor does God lower Himself below anyone. The Latin prefix *Omni* (all-encompassing) rightly describes His being, and from it, we conclude everything flows from Him, and everything is directed by Him. Every good and perfect gift,[48] every spiritual blessing,[49] and everything we need

---

46   1 John 5:10
47   Thomas Watson, *A Body of Divinity* (Carlisle, PA: Banner of Truth Trust, 2015), 12.
48   James 1:17
49   Ephesians 1:3

for life and godliness[50] come from Him. Not a molecule is out of place in this universe, and there is not a thing God has not given.[51] God rules over all. His dominion is over all the earth and everything He has made, and from Him all else flows. That alone is worthy of every praise.

The acts of God deserve our praise as well, and the greatest among them is our salvation. In Ephesians 2, Paul begins by reminding the Ephesians of their former state, that they were dead in sin. He reminds them that they were "by nature children of wrath, like the rest of mankind."[52] He then introduces the most beautiful of all the gospel words: "But God, being rich in mercy...made us alive together with Christ."[53] Paul, again, uses this wording after describing them as once "having no hope and without God in the world;"[54] "But now in Christ Jesus you who once were far off have been brought near by the blood of Christ."[55] The statement, "but God," summarizes the glory of God in salvation. It contrasts the inability of man with the ability of God. It displays God's sovereignty and dominion over all things, and His redemptive work in sinful man.

Praise is the proper response to God's sovereign work of salvation in us because it is the recognition of His glory. The natural man does not and cannot praise God. He may set up a façade of praise, but since his praise does not flow from a regenerated heart, it is not acceptable to God. True and acceptable praise flows forth from the fount of Christ in us. Such is Paul's crescendo: "Not a result of works so that no one can boast."[56] This praise is certainly in Paul's mind when he repeats, "to the

---

50   2 Peter 1:3
51   Romans 11:33-36
52   Ephesians 2:3
53   Ephesians 2:4-5
54   Ephesians 2:12
55   Ephesians 2:13
56   Ephesians 2:9

praise of His glory," numerous times while listing the blessings of our salvation in chapter one.[57]

Jesus takes it one step further when He taught God works in us to cause others to praise His glory, also.[58] By the good works He works in us, man's praise is directed away from us and toward Himself. The praise of God sets God higher than man and displays to the world His magnificence, and that is the point of praise; it does not add anything to God but exalts Him in the eyes of those around us.

In praising God's glory, we benefit our souls. C.S. Lewis considered the greatest enjoyments of life are found in what we praise. He believed we could not fully enjoy the beauty of a lover if we did not praise their beauty, nor could we fully enjoy the magnificence of nature if we kept silent.[59] When we praise God, we not only glorify Him, but we enjoy Him.

HOW DO WE PRAISE GOD?

If we go back to the the Lord's Prayer, Jesus seems to rank our petitions in order of importance. Hallowing God, or esteeming God as most blessed, revered, and praised, must be our attitude towards God throughout all praise and prayer, which means it must saturate our lives. We do not, therefore, come to Him in a light-hearted manner as a friend comes to a friend, but we come to Him in reverence and praise.

Some may object to this on the basis of Hebrews 4:16, which tells us to come to the throne of grace with boldness and confidence. Let me, however, pose two questions: How are we able to come with boldness, and why do we come to God's

---

57   Ephesians 1:3-14
58   Matthew 5:16
59   C.S. Lewis, *Reflections on the Psalms* (London ENG: Geoffrey Bles, 1958), 95.

throne? As to the first, the answer the writer of Hebrews gives is we come to the throne with boldness because we have received mercy in Christ. As to the second, the reason we come is we need mercy to persevere to the end. If this is the case, the mediating work of Christ and our need to receive mercy and grace must never cause our boldness to turn into irreverence.

We are also taught by Christ true worship is to worship God in spirit and in truth.[60] In regards to praise, this means the praise of God is both simple and centred on the Word of God. To praise God in spirit is to do away with all sorts of laws, rituals, and aesthetics of worship. Spiritual worship does not allow for distractions such as the entertainment of modern celebrity Christianity, icons of the Roman Catholic or Eastern Orthodox Churches, or any other man-made distractions. To praise God in truth, His Word must inform and direct our praise; we sing truth, read truth, hear truth, and walk in truth. Therefore, to praise God in spirit and truth requires us to be grounded and saturated in Scripture.

When we understand the reasons why we must praise God, we will better understand how we must praise Him. Theologians often use a simple phrase to describe this idea: theology leads to doxology. Because praise is the recognition of the glory of God, our praise and work to glorify God are woven tightly together. Let us, then, praise God for who He is and what He has done, and in doing so, join with the endless chorus of saints and angels already praising Him in heaven.

BOASTING IN GOD

Growing up, I loved to watch various sports on television. I still do, but as a young boy, I was drawn to certain players by how

---

60   John 4:24

they played. Yet, what they said in post-game interviews seemed to really determine whether I liked them or not. With the advent of live televised games, journalists grabbed the opportunity to catch the immediate, raw and unadulterated reaction from the players after games. Many players I watched began with saying something along the lines of, "I just want to thank God for giving me the ability to play well." These players stuck out to me, and I admired them for their courage to say something so bold on national television.

As I grew older, I began to notice something else. While many began with a God honouring statement, the rest of their interview was spent heaping praise on themselves and their teammates. Although they started by crediting God for their abilities, they placed the crown upon their own heads by boasting of all the hard work they had done to get to that spot. It was rare to see a humble perspective toward the hard work put into the sport. You know, the kind that details the hard work, yet realizes that none of it would have been effective if God was not gracious to them. When I saw their pride through the thin veneer of humility, coupled with their outward displays of ungodly living, I began to see while they honoured God with their lips, their hearts were far from Him. This may not be the case for all athletes, but it was a common theme, and I started to question whether players really meant what they said when they thanked God. This observation, however, is not only reserved for professional athletes, but it is also directed towards Christians.

Christians are prone to the same fault as many of these athletes. They give God glory with their lips while living in a way that glorifies self. Take, for instance, the popularity of verses such as Ephesians 2:8-9, which clearly state how salvation is worked out by God in such a way that no one can boast. How many other verses state the same truth! Yet, ask these Christians how they became a Christian, or how to grow as a Christian, and their answer is something other than the gospel. They heap praises on their actions as though they got the ball rolling, they were the ones seeking, and they are the reason they matured. The same can be seen in their instructions to others for maturity in faith: "You must try harder, pray more, do this, don't do that, and much more!" While many of their prescriptions for salvation and maturity are actions we must perform, a right understanding of Scripture will have us asking if we are able to perform them properly.

The apostle Paul has an answer for us in his epistle to the Philippians, "…work out your own salvation with fear and trembling, for it is God who works in you, both to will and to work for his good pleasure."[61] Paul's answer is simple: if God does not work, our work is in vain. If God does not give the increase, what use are planting and watering?[62] God must work for our work to be effective.

Why has God made salvation to be like this?

It is for His glory. It is so no one can boast in themselves. It is so Christ might be preeminent in all things.[63] Salvation is an act of God's free mercy towards undeserving sinners, so He receives the glory. He has also made spiritual growth dependent on Himself, for the same reason. To summarize our practical response to God's unmerited favour, Paul asks a rhetorical question to the Christians in Corinth, "What do you have that you did not receive?"[64] Knowing they would come to the obvious answer, he reprimands them, "If then you received it, why do you boast as if you did not receive it?"[65]

---

61   Philippians 2:12-13
62   1 Corinthians 3:7
63   Colossians 1:18
64   1 Corinthians 4:7
65   1 Corinthians 4:7

Let that question sit for a while. Do you boast in your salvation as though you didn't receive it?

To be saved, you must go to the source of salvation. You must go to the fount of Christ, which never runs dry. You cannot be holy on your own, so make haste and run to God. It is a fool's errand to try harder to do better. When you go to Christ, you will believe in God as He has been pleased to reveal Himself, particularly in Christ; then, your praise will be properly directed; then, you will boast in God; and then your salvation in Christ will honour and glorify God. Christians glorify God by recognizing Him as the source of all good in their lives.

CHAPTER THREE

The Glory of
God in Sanctification

ALTHOUGH CHRISTIANS MAKE MUCH OF THEIR SALVATION (FOR A good reason), the majority of their lives are lived in sanctification. The new birth is an event that changes the course of life, but spiritual growth is the road. Thomas Watson saw this road of sanctification as a path with many layers and aspects working together to make it passable. Sanctification, Watson affirmed, is supernatural, intrinsic, extensive, intense and ardent, beautiful, abiding, and progressive.[66] In other words, sanctification is an active (intensive and ardent) work of God (supernatural) in the heart (intrinsic) that spreads through the whole person (extensive), helping the believer persevere (abiding), and causing the believer to grow (progressive) in holiness (beautiful). Peter summarized it this way in his second epistle: "His divine power has granted to us all things that pertain to life and godliness, through the knowledge of him *who called us to his own glory and excellence.*"[67] Sanctification is God's glory and excellence in us. Here we receive true meaning in that this new reality includes everything

---

66   Watson expounds on each of these points in *A Body of Divinity*. (Watson, Thomas, *A Body of Divinity* [Carlisle, PA: Banner of Truth Trust, 2015], 241-242).

67   2 Peter 1:3 emphasis added.

we need in this life and the next, it also brings purpose in that God calls us to His service. Sanctification, then, not only glorifies God, but it enhances every endeavour for meaningful purpose.

Because of sin, the possibility of deceiving ourselves and others in matters of spiritual growth cannot be overlooked. Watson provides us with some examples of counterfeit sanctification: moral virtue, superstition, hypocrisy, and mistakenly relying on God's restraining grace and common grace as proof of God's special favour.[68] Essentially, counterfeit sanctification includes outward actions with no inward desire, empty rituals,[69] claiming to be more holy than what is true, and trusting the common grace of God that restrains men from doing as much evil as they are capable of doing and blesses unbelievers with good things for common life to save them in the end.

Explaining sanctification according to the Bible and observing its many counterfeits narrows down the practical outworking of sanctification in our lives. That, however, doesn't free us from obligation. There are still practical ways we actively glorify God in sanctification, and, according to Thomas Watson, they are confessing sin, working out our salvation, living a holy life, and bearing fruit.

CONFESSING OUR SIN

In my estimation, most Christians understand in order to be forgiven of sin, they must confess their sin. Yet, many remain ignorant as to what true confession looks like; that is, many Christians don't know how to glorify God in their confession.

---

68   Thomas Watson, *A Body of Divinity* (Carlisle, PA: Banner of Truth Trust, 2015), 242-244.
69   The rituals Watson had in mind were the rituals of the Roman Catholic Church, rituals such as using beads to pray, bowing to images, and sprinkling with holy water.

Because of pride, it is not difficult to condemn others for the same actions we condone for ourselves; we are quick to justify our actions while denouncing others who do those same actions. We dislike and even mourn our bad habits, but we do not seek to overcome them with the rigour we expect from others to overcome their problems. All this is individuality and it is pride. It sets the individual above everyone else and inevitably causes a sense of superiority to rise within. If a church adopts this mentality, they create a hostile environment for people to confess their sins to one another. Christians who attend these churches fear an ungracious response or a breach of confidentiality; they fear proud people treating them carelessly.

Why is it important for the church to be a place where one can come to confess? In 1935, Dietrich Bonhoeffer moved to Finkenwalde, where, in emergency-built houses, he took charge of a seminary to train young men for pastoral and evangelistic ministry. At his lead, it became more a school of discipleship for the young men than a school of rigorous theological study (although that was included) because his goal was to create a place where they all could devote themselves to the Christian community. Three years later, Bonhoeffer documented and published his observations and biblical insights from their time together in a book entitled, *Gemeinsames Leben,* later translated into English as *Life Together.*[70] The book was not at all meant to tell Christians how to do church but to explain why the Christian community needed to include every ordinance Scripture commands of them in church life. Regarding the confession of sin, Bonhoeffer observed for the majority of life, a person could only truly confess their sin if they confessed to a brother or a sister.[71] Most of the

---

70   Dietrich Bonhoeffer, Life Together [New York, NY: HarperOne, 1954] 10-11
71   For further explanation, read Bonhoeffer's observations in chapter five of *Life To-gether.* (Dietrich Bonhoeffer, *Life Together* [New York, NY: HarperOne, 1954]).

private confessions before God, he found, were only confessions to one's self. They were not honest confessions that brought sin to light. Personally, I think there is some merit to his claim. In 1 John 1:5-10, John speaks of confessing our sin as an act of walking in the light, which means our sin can only be forgiven by God when it comes to light. Of course, this may happen in the prayer closet, but the greatest certainty of an honest confession comes within the confidence of another person. By honestly confessing our sin to another, we are helped in our confession to God.

One of the great paradoxes in Christian life is a sincere and honest confession exalts God. When we confess our sin simply and honestly, we place all the blame on ourselves. Our confession condemns us before God because we acknowledge the fact sin originates in our hearts, not in our reaction to circumstances, surroundings, and other's actions. It condemns us because we confess our acts of sin closely agree with our hearts. We do not confess as Adam did. He did not deny his sin, but instead of placing the blame on himself, he directed it toward God through directing it to Eve. Nor do we confess by contrasting our sin with some good deed to mitigate our condemnation. True confession places all the blame on one's self.

God is glorified in an honest and sincere confession because it clears God of all blame in the sight of others. When confession properly places the blame on ourselves, it clears God of any fault and exalts His holiness and righteousness; it declares before God there is no sin found in Him; it declares sin is found in us and it is very much a part of us; it declares the problem lies within us and not with God. This kind of confession is true because it can never be forced. To proclaim God is holy and just in His character and actions cannot come from the natural man, but from a heart made able by the Holy Spirit. True confession is a work of

God because the light is the only way the deeds in the darkness can be revealed.

God's grace is also magnified in true confession. Since the basic definition of grace is unmerited favour and there is nothing we can do to receive it, we have no manipulative control over it. God gives grace, and He gives to whomever He will. When we come under the impression God's grace is given to "good people," we put ourselves in a place where grace will not be given. All our striving to receive grace by giving a partial confession, hiding certain sin from God, or attempting to appear perfect hinders that very grace from being applied. God is glorified in giving grace to those who deserve the worst condemnation. The thief on the cross, though he lived a life as an enemy of God, found grace by a sincere confession in his final moment of life. Christians find comfort in a sincere confession because of the words of Paul, "…where sin increased, grace abounded all the more."[72]

Our confession must be true and sincere to glorify God. If we are to expect grace to forgive us and cleanse us from all unrighteousness, we must bring our sin to light before God. We must approach God as the prodigal son approached his father. He blamed himself before his father did, and he blamed himself as the sole perpetrator of his sinful actions. That kind of confession glorifies God.

WORKING OUT OUR SALVATION

Another paradoxical way we glorify God is by working out our salvation. It is paradoxical in the practical sense because we further our good, particularly our eternal happiness, while at the same time furthering God's glory in us and in this world. In the gospel sense, we work out the salvation given to us, not because

---

72   Romans 5:20

of our works but because we did not work.[73] To make matters more complicated, understanding the relationship between our good works and salvation is a delicate path to travel; too much to one side, and everyone lands in the ditch.

This tension, however, is not uncommon in biblical doctrine. In most cases, tension arises because our fleshly desires war with scriptural authority. Primarily, however, the tension here is between parallel doctrines.

Paul wades through the complexity, clarifying these parallel truths in Philippians 2:12-13. He tells us to "work out our salvation with fear and trembling, for it is God who works in us to will and to do his good pleasure." First, we are told we must work which sounds simple enough. To be told to work is not the problem since it is part of sanctification as Paul tells us in another place we are to walk in the good works which God has prepared beforehand,[74] and James, who teaches faith must produce works to prove itself genuine.[75]

The problem is introduced immediately following Paul's exhortation to work out our salvation: God is the one working His will and purpose in us as we work. God working is not the problem either; the problem is how our work relates to His work. Our fundamental problem is our sinful nature's unwillingness to cooperate with God, and it shows up in two ways. We might say, "If God is working, I no longer have to work." That is a problem. Or, we might dismiss God's work and focus on our ability to work. That is also a problem. The answer to our problems is found in a little word located in the middle of Paul's exhortation. If we do not pay attention to it, or if we do not understand its importance, we miss Paul's entire point. It is the

---

73   Romans 4:5
74   Ephesians 2:10
75   James 2:26

word "for." The simple use of this word is to show the reader what *has been said* is built upon what *will be said*. Here, its use is to display the foundation of our work, and by it, we learn why we must work, how we can work, and why we work with fear and trembling—rather than weariness, or joy, or fervour.

The reason we work is God works. God entangles our work with His work for the purpose of glorifying Him, and His work is the decisive factor in ours. His work is good, not ours and that makes our work meaningful, effective, and pleasing to Him. We glorify God when we work because His work through us accomplished His will. God does what we were incapable of doing, yet commanded to do. And this works its way into why we work with "fear and trembling." It is because the Almighty, Sovereign God of the universe is at work in us.

Many who attempt to hold both these truths at the same time often lean to one side or the other. Those who place more emphasis on morality will place more emphasis on working out their salvation. Those less inclined to work will place more emphasis on God's work. Our practical problem usually tends to focus on our work and not on God's. Either we try our best to perform at the level which only God's power can achieve, or we rely on a misconstrued idea of grace and forget the good works we are called to do. The way in which Paul goes about it, however, is far too liberal for the morally minded and far too moral for the liberal-minded. He maintains all our good works cannot appease God unless God works. There is no room here for any reliance on our abilities to present something of worth or value to God. Likewise, he maintains we *must* produce good works. The work of God displays itself in our good works, calling us towards higher moral standards—grace produces nothing less.

As recorded in Matthew's gospel, Jesus compared His followers to lamps. He commanded them, "Let your light shine before others so they may see your good works, and give glory to your Father who is in heaven."[76] We work out our salvation publicly in such a way that God is glorified by it. As light is foreign to darkness, we are foreigners in this world, displaying the fruit of our glorious homeland. Our good works shine in this dark world to display our Father's mercy.

Then we come to the initial paradox: as we work for the glory of God, we harvest the fruit of joy from our labours. Obedience to God's Word causes us to do good in this world, to be kind to others, faithful, and self-controlled. We enjoy the fruit of a peaceful and happy life in God. What is more, our joy in Christ increases as we grow in fellowship with Him. In the spiritual realm, working out our salvation causes us to live for something more than this life offers.

Thomas Watson compared Christians to subjects of a kind prince, willing to serve him at all costs:

> Would it not be an encouragement to a subject, to hear his prince say to him, "'You will honor and please me very much, if you will go to yonder mine of gold, and dig as much gold for yourself as you can carry away"? So, for God to say, "Go to the ordinances, get as much grace as you can, dig out as much salvation as you can; and the more happiness you have, the more I shall count myself glorified!"[77]

HOLY LIVING

Holiness is vital to the Christian faith; it is the encompassing definition of the Christian life. The God whom we serve, to

---

76   Matthew 5:16
77   Thomas Watson, *A Body of Divinity* (Carlisle, PA: Banner of Truth Trust, 2015), 14.

whom we are bound in Christ, demands holiness of us because He is holy.[78] He demands it of His own because they are His children, and as His children, they must look like Him. He makes them holy by setting them apart, and requires they act according to their position in Him. Further, because God is holy, He blesses the holy and curses the unholy. The first place most think to look for holiness is in the Old Testament, where God's commands for holy living are most prominent. But holiness is not confined to the Old Testament, the New Testament speaks much of the subject, and clarifies it in light of Christ.

> Even as he chose us in him before the foundation of the world, that we should be holy and blameless before him. In love he predestined us for adoption to himself as sons through Jesus Christ, according to the purpose of his will, to the praise of his glorious grace, with which he has blessed us in the Beloved.[79]

Paul ties the topic of holiness with our salvation, clarifying salvation gives birth to holiness. He doesn't stop there. He goes way back—too far for us to comprehend—to when there was nothing but God. There, God had a plan for salvation, to save certain people in order that they would be holy. While it is true this salvation was not a reality in us until we believed in Jesus, the plan always existed.

To progress in understanding how God makes us holy, we need to understand the doctrine of election. To do that, I must first address the fact the truth Paul wrote of in this one small verse has faced much opposition since the time of Christ. It is arguably the most despised doctrine in the history of the church.

---

78   1 Peter 1:16
79   Ephesians 1:4-6

Some label it a doctrine of demons, but most are content to be-lieve it to be unbecoming of a loving God. They invent straw men to refute this doctrine. The first is the man who desperately wants to be saved but cannot because God has not chosen him, and the second is the man who hates God and never wants to be saved, but since he is chosen, he is saved against his will. Both of these are false. There are no such people to fit the description of these two men. You will never find a person who desperately wishes he was elect who is not, nor will you find a person who is elect yet desperately wishes he wasn't.

Why? The answer is sin. Sin so corrupts us that we want nothing to do with God in the first place. We gladly and free-ly choose sin every single time, sometimes even in the form of good works. We are naturally servants of sin who faithfully and joyfully serve our master. We cannot choose God. God, by free grace and mercy, removes the natural heart of sin in the elect and replaces it with a heart able to choose what is truly good.[80] He rescues us from the master of sin and makes righteousness our master.[81]

Because the doctrine of election is clearly presented in the Bible, those who despise it must still deal with it. One of the more popular arguments is because of God's foreknowledge of every happening, God looked down the corridor of time to see who would accept his offer of salvation and chose those peo-ple.[82] In other words, they argue the elect are those who God foresaw would accept Christ and bear the fruit of holiness. Con-trary to this argument, Paul argues, "Even as [God] chose us in

---

80 Ezekiel 11:19, 36:26
81 Romans 6:18
82 The reason they believe God looks at man's choice before choosing them is be-cause they believe God gives everyone the same opportunity (prevenient grace) to be saved. That, however, leaves us in the same place as before where we choose holiness before God chooses us. In the Bible, God's electing grace is always spo-ken of as effective in producing what it set out to do (i.e. holiness).

[Christ] before the foundation of the world, *that we should be holy and blameless* before [God]."[83] God did indeed see us before the world began, but what He saw was sinful people with nothing to cause Him to love. Because God elected us of His grace and mercy, holiness is a product of election and not the cause of it.

A few years ago, I taught this passage in Ephesians to my church's youngest youth group (aged 12-14) to help them understand God's salvation. To explain election, I used a simple analogy, a scenario in which I had five imaginary bottles of their favourite pop. In this scenario, I would choose five of the youth at random to whom I would give these imaginary bottles. Immediately, they all raised their hands, asking me to pick them. When I had selected five of the youth, the rest were noticeably disappointed in me and thought I was unfair, which was an honest response for someone that age (especially when pop is involved!). I explained how many of us view God as being unfair in only choosing some, not all, to salvation. The only problem is we forget we don't deserve to be saved. Although many of them thought they deserved a bottle of pop, no one ever deserves to be saved, and that is the point of it all. God saves us by His mercy alone. It is all mercy, and the point of election is to prove it to the greatest extent.

Why do I trouble you with the doctrine of election when dealing with the subject of holiness? Because Paul does, and he does so for a particular reason. God doesn't just receive glory when we live lives separate from the pattern of the world; He receives glory by our holiness because He is the cause of it. He takes us out of the world so we might live for Him and not ourselves. God is magnified when we live our lives in a different way than those around us, but what is often forgotten is God is also magnified when we acknowledge Him as the source of our

---

83   Ephesians 1:4, emphasis added.

holiness. After all, the overarching purpose of election to holy and blameless lives is "to the praise of his glorious grace."[84]

BEAR FRUIT

A life of holiness is a fruitful life. To merely profess faith is not proof of genuine faith nor does it glorify God, but it is the fruit of faith that proves it genuine and so glorifies God. Of course, producing Christian fruit does not require every Christian everywhere to work in a vineyard or orchard, but it would certainly help if we all became a little acquainted with how they work. Fruit is a rather brilliant picture because it describes many aspects of Christian life instead of only one, and each one helps us to understand how to glorify God by it.

In John's gospel, Jesus uses an illustration of a vineyard to teach His disciples about growth in their holiness, and He intertwines God's glory with the production of fruit. "By this my Father is glorified, that you bear much fruit…"[85] He likens Himself to a vine and His disciples to the branches. The point of this was simple: Jesus was explaining that apart from Him, those who follow Him accomplish nothing. In the picture of the vine, branches only bear fruit if they are connected to a source of nutrients, or else they wither and die. If Jesus is the true vine, branches that wish to produce good and true fruit must be connected to Him.

The perennial problem of many Christians is self-dependency to produce this fruit efficiently. Take, for instance, how I often heard the fruit of the Spirit taught and applied in my younger years. Love, joy, peace, patience, etc. were addressed as things that must be worked for to obtain. We were told we must

---

84   Ephesians 1:6
85   John 15:8

get them by striving for them. But, if this is our approach, we have missed the mark. Paul is not teaching some sort of Christian morality but speaks of fruit in the same way Jesus spoke of it. A fruitful life is a supernatural life because it obtains everything necessary for life and godliness from Christ and not from a concentrated effort. We do not look inward for the strength to love others, nor do we practice rituals and meditations to obtain peace and joy because *the fruit of the Holy Spirit comes from the Holy Spirit.*

A Basic Definition of Fruit

Fruit is organic. When we plant a tree, it does not immediately produce fruit, nor should we expect to pick ripe fruit from it the next day. We also cannot watch fruit grow in real time; it takes time for an apple tree to produce ripe apples. So it is with Christian fruitfulness, we do not obtain every good fruit of the Holy Spirit immediately. We must be fed and watered by the Word of God and have our unfruitful branches pruned through trials.

Fruit is also a direct representation of the health of its source. It shows us the health of the roots and of the vine. That is why in Gardening 101 if you want to produce good fruit, you pay little attention to the fruit itself. What use is it to paint and shine up bad fruit on a tree? The tree will only continue to produce bad fruit. When you deal with the health of the vine and make the roots healthy, good fruit will naturally be the result. The vine of the Christian life is Christ, who is pure and blameless, so bad fruit is not a result of the health of the vine, but the result of a branch no longer attached to the vine. Indeed, there is no possibility of us producing the fruit of the Spirit unless we abide in Christ.

Two points of application are drawn from this illustration. First, we must abide in Christ if we want to live fruitful lives.

Abiding in Christ is not merely attending church regularly, reading a devotion each morning, and praying each evening. It is that, but it is much more. It recognizes the self as dead apart from the life-giving nutrients of Christ. Church attendance, Bible reading, and prayer are the means by which we abide in Christ, but without the foundation of total dependence on Christ, each means will be of no value.

Second, we must grow with patience. In a time and place such as we live today where instant is expected, patience is not seen as a virtue. Often, our thinking follows this line, "If I have not overcome my vices and shortcomings by the end of the day through abiding in Christ, I will just do it myself!" From the beginning, however, Christian growth in fruitfulness was never meant to be completed before we die. Through seasons of plenty and seasons of want, we must bear fruit our entire life, growing into a mature branch.

This sanctification glorifies God because it is a supernatural work. As Thomas Watson notes, our sanctification is special and should be treated as such.

> Are there any here that are sanctified? God has done more for you than millions, who may be illumined, but are not sanctified. He has done more for you than if he had made you the sons of princes, and caused you to ride upon the high places of the earth. Are you sanctified? Heaven is begun in you; for happiness is nothing but the quintessence of holiness. Oh, how thankful should you be to God![86]

Therefore, we glorify God in our sanctification most when we most rely on His power and work within us.

---

86   Thomas Watson, *A Body of Divinity* (Carlisle, PA: Banner of Truth Trust, 2015), 250.

CHAPTER FOUR

The Glory of God Through His Own to the World

AS THE CHRISTIAN PRODUCES GOOD FRUIT, THE WORLD NOTICES. But the world also notices when the Christian calls it to turn to Christ. That call is a proclamation for all tribes, tongues, and nations to join Christ and live lives that glorify God. Christians are commanded not only to show the world the glory of God in their salvation and growth in holiness, but to glorify God in sharing the gospel.

Sharing the gospel glorifies God because it displays to the watching world God is worthy of our lives and worship. It glorifies God because it stands up against the enemies of God. It glorifies God because it turns enemies of God into children of God.

CONTENDING FOR THE TRUTH

When Friedrich Nietzsche famously remarked that God had died and modern society was to blame, he could just as well have claimed truth died the same way.

> Truth is dead. Truth remains dead, and we have killed it. How can we console ourselves, the most murderous of

all murderers? What was holiest and mightiest of all the world has yet possessed has bled to death under our knives: who will wipe this blood off us? With what water could we clean ourselves? What standard, what teaching shall we have to invent? Is not the greatness of this deed too great for us? Must we ourselves not become the ones who determine truth simply to appear worthy of it?[87]

There is a connection between the death of God and the death of truth. When God dies in the minds of a society, absolute truth dies as well. If there is no Author of truth, everyone becomes their own author, their own god. So, if we contend for the truth, we contend for God.

To convey the task of contending for the truth, Thomas Watson uses the phrase, "standing up for truth." He compares it to a servant caring for his master's goods: "God has intrusted us with his truth, as a master intrusts his servant with his purse to keep."[88] When we care for God's truth as a servant cares for his master's purse, we glorify God. In our contention for the truth we face the problem of those who claim God's truth isn't worthy of contention, that it has no value, and doesn't exist. Yet, we must stand up for it regardless of our opposition.

---

87 The original words of Nietzsche: "God is dead. God remains dead. And we have killed him. How can we console ourselves, the murderers of all murderers? The holiest and mightiest thing the world has ever possessed has bled to death under our knives: who will wipe this blood from us? With what water could we clean ourselves? What festivals of atonement, what holy games will we have to invent for ourselves? Is the magnitude of this deed not too great for us? Do we not ourselves have to become gods merely to appear worthy of it?" (Friedrich Nietzsche, *The Gay Science* [Cambridge, UK: Cambridge University Press, 2001], 120).

88 Thomas Watson, *A Body of Divinity* (Carlisle, PA: Banner of Truth Trust, 2015), 15.

Created in His Image

We are created in the image of God, the Author of truth, and the understanding divine truth exists is imbedded within us. We are created to seek truth, and our longing is to know it. Since sin is in our nature, we look for it in all the wrong places, but because there is no truth apart from Him, all the other sources we sinfully trust soon show their true colours in their lies and contradictions. God's truth is absolute, so we won't find absolute truth apart from His Word. Recognizing this is the first step when contending for truth.

The Word of God is our rule for life, and within it is everything we need for both this life and the next. Paul tells the Romans they cannot advance in the Christian life unless they first hear the Word of God.[89] It is not enough just to hear God's Word, but it is the necessary first step of contending for truth. Recognizing God's truth as absolute means we are compelled to submit to it, obey it, and love it when we hear it. If those actions don't follow hearing, we don't recognize God's truth as truth.

Compelled to Contend

When a soldier loves his country, he will do whatever it takes to protect it; he will contend for it. In the same way, Christians do whatever it takes to stand up for God's truth. Jude expresses the way a Christian does this:

> Beloved, although I was very eager to write to you about our common salvation, I found it necessary to write appealing to you to contend for the faith that was once for all delivered to the saints. For certain people have crept in unnoticed who

---

89   Romans 10:17

43

long ago were designated for this condemnation, ungodly people, who pervert the grace of our God into sensuality and deny our only Master and Lord, Jesus Christ.[90]

The Greek word used here for contend indicates contention for something with great effort. It means to compete against or oppose a thing with great force. Paul says much the same thing to the Corinthians: "We destroy arguments and every lofty opinion raised against the knowledge of God, and take every thought captive to obey Christ."[91]

John Calvin (1509-1564) once wrote in a letter to the Queen of Navarre, explaining the reason he opposed a certain group of people, "A dog barks and stands at bay if he sees any one assault his master. I should be indeed remiss, if, seeing the truth of God thus attacked, I should remain dumb, without giving one note of warning."[92] When we hear God's truth and submit to it, we will contend for it.

God doesn't let philosophy, experience-based belief, or sin overrun His church because He raises up faithful servants who contend for truth. One of the early contenders for truth was Athanasius of Alexandria (296-373). Athanasius took a lone stand for God's truth and received the moniker, *Athanasius Contra Mundum* (Athanasius Against the World). Continuing in this tradition, God has raised up servants to defend truth and correct the church so its sights are reset to the path of truth. The lesson we learn from the great men and women who stood for truth, and those who stand for truth today is oftentimes we will stand alone. Jude's warning of the church falling into many errors

---

90   Jude 1:3-4
91   2 Corinthians 10:5
92   John Calvin, *Tracts and Letters, Volume Four* (Carlisle, PA: Banner of Truth Trust, 2009), 454.

where Christians don't contend for God's truth encourages us to persevere.

While Jude gives warning to the church as a collection, Paul gives warning to the individual. His warning is if we do not contend for truth, we may make shipwreck of our faith. Our faith is rooted in the truth of which Christ bears witness,[93] and if our faith is not rooted in Christ, it lacks the necessary nutrients to flourish. It will wither and die without truth. Therefore, not only is the church liable to gross sin when Christians fail to contend for the truth, but individual Christians are as well. We must be lovers of truth, and as lovers of the truth, ardent contenders for it.

Are you willing to be as Athanasius and stand against the world? Are you willing to stand up for truth and contend for it? Your faith and the well-being of your church depend on it. More than that, the glory of God in this world is at stake, because where His truth is contended for and upheld, there His glory shines forth into the darkness.

EVANGELISM

To contend against those who oppose God's truth is only part of the Christian's duty to glorify God in this world, and as important as it is to have an airtight and strong grasp of truth, it is just as important to proclaim the goodness of God's truth to everyone. Christians have a positive message to share with the world, a message of good news. In evangelism, Christians call the world to Christ through sharing the gospel. Thomas Watson again put it this way: "We should be both diamonds and loadstones, diamonds for the lustre of grace, and loadstones for

---

93   John 18:37

attractive virtue in drawing others to Christ."[94] In evangelism, Christians simultaneously display the glory of God while calling others to Him.

In Mark's gospel, we read of Jesus crossing over to the other side of Galilee. What seems at first as an insignificant voyage to our modern perspective was a significant journey in that time because He crossed over to a place no Jewish person wished to go. It is immediately made apparent why. When they get to the other side, Jesus and the disciples meet a man possessed by unclean spirits living among the tombs. Jesus casts the unclean spirits out of the man, but they beg not to be cast out of the country. So Jesus commanded them to enter a herd of pigs, which, when possessed, immediately ran off the nearby cliff into the sea. Perhaps it is a peculiar question in light of the monumental act of Jesus casting out demons, but what would pigs be doing anywhere near a Jewish town? Or better yet, what sane farmer would think he could make a profit on raising pigs in a Jewish land? The herd of pigs is our clue Jesus was no longer in Jewish territory. Jesus was now in the land of the Gentiles, and He had just performed a miracle there.

The townspeople heard rumblings of an extraordinary event and came out to see for themselves what had happened. When they arrived, they found a man they all knew as dangerous and untameable now clothed, calm, and seated by Jesus. As Mark recounts to us, they begged Jesus to leave that region. I am not sure exactly why they begged Jesus to leave, but it could have been they were afraid of the light Jesus brought, as John wrote, "And this is the judgment...people loved the darkness rather than the light because their works are evil."[95] It is possible

---

94   Loadstone is another word for magnet. (Thomas Watson, *A Body of Divinity* [Carlisle, PA: Banner of Truth Trust, 2015], 16).
95   John 3:19

they feared the darkness of their hearts and their deeds being exposed for all to see. Regardless of their reasons, the events that happen next makes this story astounding.

As Jesus and His disciples prepared to leave, the man Jesus had just freed from the unclean spirits asked to come along. Jesus answered him in a way He had never answered before. "Go home and tell them what the Lord has done for you."[96] Before this event, whenever Jesus healed someone or performed a miracle, He commanded them not to tell anyone. Now He had something different in mind. Mark tells us the man went and proclaimed the work of Christ in all the cities of the area.

We don't see the fruit of this work until three chapters later, when Jesus is back in this same region, called Decapolis. The response of the people is radically different from the previous time. Now they brought every sick person they could find for Jesus to heal. This was, as far as we know, the result of one man proclaiming and showing the glorious work of Christ.

While Jesus was there, Mark records about four thousand people gathered to hear Him preach. They were hungry, and Jesus had compassion on them. Someone in the crowd brought seven loaves of bread that day, so Jesus took the loaves and performed His second miracle of multiplying food. By this miracle, Jesus displayed to the Gentiles He was the bread of life not only to the Jews (in feeding the five thousand) but also now to the Gentiles. The apostle Paul explains Christ's actions in his letter to the Romans when he tells us the gospel "is the power of God for salvation to everyone who believes, to the Jew first and also to the Greek."[97] He continues through the entire letter of Romans, weaving the gospel through the Jews and Gentiles, showing them Christ is their common salvation and their reason for

---

96   Mark 5:19
97   Romans 1:16

unity. Jesus and Paul teach us evangelism reaches people all over the world regardless of tribe, tongue, and nation.

We must be as this Gentile man and go into all the world with the message of Christ, labouring to bring others to Him. We go into a world that does not want to know Jesus, a world much the same as the region of Decapolis—lovers of darkness— and we labour for the good news of Christ. Our aim in this labour is to be as a diamond, displaying to all the world the glory of God and the joy He brings, and like a magnet, drawing and persuading many to Christ by the Word of God. When those who once loved darkness, heading toward hell, and under sin's hold are snatched from that pathway and set on the pathway of life and light, God is glorified.

PASSIONATE CHRISTIANITY

The tie which binds every Christian endeavours to glorify God in this world is a burning desire to see it happen. Passion for the glory of God drives Christians to glorify God. Without it, Christians not only become complacent in their evangelism, but they also show the world what they are living for isn't all that great. Passionless Christianity is a misnomer. Nowhere in Scripture do we find God condoning people for lacking passion. In fact, we find the opposite. We find God commanding passion from His people and condemning passionless service.

Passion, or zeal, is a double affection for something or someone. It is love and hatred working together for one purpose. To an extent, we are always passionate people, in that when we love someone or even something, we inevitably hate all that which is against it. I have heard many say the enemy of love is hate, but it's not. The enemy of love is apathy. We must hate if we are to love. Love and hatred walk hand in hand in the union of passion.

When we apply this passion towards God, we have two steps to take. The first step is to have our affections and desires for Him *alone*. Our love will be directed to God and His glory above all else. The second step is hatred for everything against God. Our hatred will be directed toward sin and evil, and we will hate the darkness of evil.

Our trouble with this is our naturally disordered passions. Since we are born dead in sin, our desires are not for God, as Paul says, "…we all once lived in the passions of our flesh, carrying out the desires of the body and the mind…"[98] This means our natural affections, apart from the regenerating work of God, are for sin and evil. We naturally hate the light and love the darkness.[99] It does not matter if we live religious and moral lives or if we live vile and wicked lives; our natural passion is fleshly and sinful.

In Ezekiel's prophecy of regeneration by the Holy Spirit through Christ, God's salvific work deals with our problem of passion. "I will give you a new heart, and a new spirit I will put within you. And I will remove the heart of stone from your flesh and give you a heart of flesh."[100] The new heart given to us is not condemned by sin. Our new, living heart (the heart of flesh) succeeds in what our cold, dead heart (the heart of stone) failed to do. However, now that the heart of flesh is able to direct its passion towards God, we must have a spirit animating passion within it. To simply have a capacity for something is not the same as being able to fill that capacity. One can build a cistern, but that cistern does him no good if he built it during a drought. Without water, the cistern cannot be filled. So it is with our heart, once we

---

98   Ephesians 2:3
99   John 3:19
100   Ezekiel 36:26

have a new heart capable of loving and glorifying God, we need a new spirit to give us a continued desire to love and glorify God. Therefore, Ezekiel continues in the next verse, "And I will put my Spirit within you, and cause you to walk in my statutes and be careful to obey my rules."[101]

As Christians, a battle still wages in our passions. Directing our passions toward God does not come automatically or easily. We do not fight against flesh and blood, says the apostle Paul, but our battle is against powers and principalities, rulers of darkness and spiritual wickedness.[102] He lists the manifestations of these sinful passions in his letter to the Galatians: idolatry, hatred, jealousy, sexual immorality, envy, and things like these.[103] These acts of passion must not characterize Christians. Instead, Christians walk according to the passion of the Holy Spirit who produces the fruit of love, joy, peace, patience, kindness, goodness, faithfulness, gentleness, and self-control.[104]

Why should we be passionate for God's glory? Because, as is the overarching point of this book, God is passionate for His glory. In the same passage of Ezekiel quoted above, we find God giving the reason why He places a new heart and a new spirit within His people. Two separate times He tells them it is not for their sake, but for the sake of His name that He acts.[105] Because God is passionate for His glory, He causes us to become passionate for it too. His passion creates our passion; His zeal fuels our zeal; His desire causes our desire. God's passion for His glory is our only hope for us to become passionate Christians. I have heard some argue God's desire for His own glory makes Him narcissistic. Contrary to the natural mind, however, God is

---

101   Ezekiel 36:27
102   Ephesians 6:12
103   Galatians 5:19-21
104   Galatians 5:22-23
105   Ezekiel 36:22, 32

not narcissistic. Who is greater that He should bow to them? No one! God must be passionate for His own glory. Otherwise, He would not be God. There is no one greater, no one higher who could demand the passion of God.

How do we attain this passion? Our old passions, as Paul clearly states, must be put to death.[106] Our natural passion for sin and evil must die for us to obtain the passion of God in Christ. Again, this happens by His Holy Spirit; by Him we will love God with all our being, and likewise, hate sin.

Do you desire to glorify God in this world? Study the truth of God's Word so you can contend for it in the marketplace of ideas and in the face of opposition. Learn the love and care of Christ for the lost, and labour for the gospel to bring light to peoples of all nations and tribes. Above all, be sure your passion for God's glory is fuelled by His Spirit.

---

106   Romans 6:1-11

CHAPTER FIVE

The Glory of
God in Suffering

CHRISTIANS DO NOT SHY AWAY FROM THE MOST DIFFICULT PARTS OF life because their lives revolve around the death and resurrection of Christ. They don't shy away because the Bible doesn't shy away from suffering. Since no one can escape the fact suffering is part of the human condition, the pressing question becomes one of dealing properly with it. There is a massive divide between the way a Christian responds to suffering and the way an unbeliever responds to suffering, and that reason is the glory of God.

CONTENT WITH THE PROVIDENTIAL HAND OF GOD

In Christian thought, the idea of God's providence finds opposition more often than acceptance because, in the end, it sets aside human autonomy. However, those who believe in God's providence, who submit to it and live by it, find themselves brought to greater heights of worship and deeper rest in Christ. Ultimately, they glorify God when they live and think in light of God's providence.

The reason many object to God's providence is found in humankind's sinful nature. Our pride hates the idea of a sovereign God who rules over us, a God who orders and ordains all that comes to pass. We don't mind a God who rules the wind and the seas, but we want nothing to do with a God who determines and orders our lives. The Bible speaks plainly about how God allots the place where man should dwell[107] and how He moves a man from one country to another.[108] Take human birth, for example. We didn't determine if we would be born, when we would be born, where we would be born, and to whom we would be born. Then, in our childhood (which influences our later years), we are completely dependent on those around us. And as we observe the course of our life from childhood to the present in our later years, we find we were (and are) more dependent than we realized.

What is the right response to God's providence found both in nature and Scripture? It is contentment. But, contentment is difficult to come by. It is no trouble for us to shake our fists at God, ignore His providence, and live as if God's providence were not true, but such an attitude does not glorify Him. Only when we are content with God's providential hand, do we glorify Him.

WHY DOES CONTENTMENT GLORIFY GOD?

When we are content with where God's providence places us, we make much of the wisdom and rule of God. Our contentment declares our belief in an all-wise God, it makes much of the sovereignty of God, and through contentment, we realize the fact that in Him we live and move and have our being.[109]

Puritan preachers spent a lot of their pulpit ministry preaching about God's providence. Their congregants did not

---

107   Acts 17:26
108   Isaiah 46:11
109   Acts 17:28

live comfortable lives in the way we do today with our homes, grocery stores, and hospitals, and they needed a sure foundation to place their feet. But comfort wasn't the only reason they focused on providence, they needed contentment too, which Thomas Watson described as living after God's own heart:

> A good Christian argues thus: It is God that has put me in this condition; he could have raised me higher, if he pleased, but that might have been a snare to me: he has done it in wisdom and love; therefore I will sit down satisfied with my condition. Surely this glorifies God much; God counts himself much honoured by such a Christian. Here, says God, is one after mine own heart; let me do what I will with him, I hear no murmuring, he is content. This shows abundance of grace.[110]

So often, we wish to be in a different place than we are currently in because we covet something "better". This is discontentment. As Christians, we truly must long for heaven—indeed pray for it to arrive quickly—but while we wait, we are confined to this life. This life is filled with disappointments and hardships, but to long for something better than where providence has placed us shows distrust towards God.

Perhaps this message means more for those in a time long gone. In our modern culture, we have abundance and the abundance of choice. To live a less-than abundant life (according to the culture's standards) means we have made poor choices, and the responsibility for it lies heavily on us. We almost cannot conceive of a providential hand carrying us along, but we likewise cannot find contentment in a world of choices. This is not to

---

110   Thomas Watson, *A Body of Divinity* (Carlisle, PA: Banner of Truth Trust, 2015),
         13.

say we must never look for better things in this life, or dream of things to accomplish, but rather we must avoid coveting. Contentment strikes coveting dead at the root, for in contentment, there is no possibility of placing any want or desire above God. Contentment in God's providence is the height of contentment in this world.

To be content in God while life is good still glorifies God because it says that God is better than even the best in this life. However, in the worst of situations, contentment glorifies God to a greater extent as Watson states, "For one to be content when he is in heaven is no wonder; but to be content under severe trials, greatly glorifies God."[111]

The apostle Paul knew severe trials more than any other:

> [I have worked] with far greater labors, far more imprisonments, with countless beatings, and often near death. Five times I received at the hands of the Jews the forty lashes less one. Three times I was beaten with rods. Once I was stoned. Three times I was shipwrecked; a night and a day I was adrift at sea; on frequent journeys, in danger from rivers, danger from robbers, danger from my own people, danger from Gentiles, danger in the city, danger in the wilderness, danger at sea, danger from false brothers; in toil and hardship, through many a sleepless night, in hunger and thirst, often without food, in cold and exposure. And, apart from other things, there is the daily pressure on me of my anxiety for all the churches.[112]

What is Paul's response to this?

---

111   Thomas Watson, *A Body of Divinity* (Carlisle, PA: Banner of Truth Trust, 2015), 13.

112   2 Corinthians 11:23-28

I will boast all the more gladly of my weaknesses, so that the power of Christ may rest upon me. For the sake of Christ, then, I am content with weaknesses, insults, hardships, persecutions, and calamities. For when I am weak, then I am strong.[113]

He found the answer to the longing of his soul in the providence of God, in the blessing of Christ. Paul saw the blessing of God's providence because He knew wherever God's hand would lead, there Christ would bless. His troubles and hardships would most likely tear any person to virtually nothing, but Paul endured through Christ, content in the place providence had set him. He was able to abound in riches or lack everything; still, he would not lose his contentment.

Such contentment greatly glorifies God, for it says of God, "Your ways are much better than my ways." It glorifies God because it displays the well which never runs dry. The one who finds such contentment shows the world that though it is lack or abundance, satisfaction is found in God alone.

THE PURPOSE OF SUFFERING

As Christ sweat drops of blood in the garden of Gethsemane, He prayed a prayer that troubles many Christians. Many pray with Christ, "let this cup pass from me," but few continue, "nevertheless, Your will be done." They are quick to wish the pain and suffering looming overhead would disappear. The pain is tough, unpleasant, a hindrance to normal life, and they would rather not experience it.

On the contrary to these natural desires, we find the New Testament teaches throughout that Christians suffer. We read

113   2 Corinthians 12:9-10

those who follow Jesus must deny themselves and pick up their cross as though they were headed to their death;[114] we read those who live a godly life will suffer;[115] we read persecution for Christ's sake should not come as a surprise;[116] we read God disciplines those He loves.[117] The suffering we face glorifies God because it is God's device to produce His good in us.

For Discipline

The writer of Hebrews encouraged believers to consider Christ and His joy in suffering. Following his encouragement, he provided the reason to persevere in suffering. "It is for discipline that you have to endure. God is treating you as sons. For what son is there whom his father does not discipline?"[118] God, as a loving Father, disciplines those He loves. He disciplines His children to correct and guide them in a fallen world. To suffer for the sake of Christ, then, is a great comfort for the Christian because it affirms we are the children of God. This affirmation is part of the New Testament principle of sonship. When we are disciplined by our Heavenly Father, we are disciplined as sons. It is not to exclude women, but to emphasize our importance to God. Ancient near-Eastern culture regarded sons as greater importance than daughters. They were given priority, and their needs mattered more than the needs of their sisters. God is not propagating such a practice when He calls us sons, but rather, He is showing us we are His priority. Sonship is about our status with God, and it means we are not an inconvenience to Him. He cares for us with great patience and kindness, allowing for

---

114   Matthew 16:24
115   2 Timothy 3:12
116   John 15:18-19
117   Hebrews 12:6
118   Hebrews 12:7

suffering to discipline us so we grow in holiness. God desires we might live, so He disciplines us for a time in order to correct us from ways that lead to death.

Our discipline may seem tough; it may hurt, it may seem to cause us damage, but the fruit of it tastes much sweeter than the finest fruit on earth. The writer of Hebrews continues his encouragement for believers facing tough times, "For the moment all discipline seems painful rather than pleasant, but later it yields the peaceful fruit of righteousness to those who have been trained by it."[119]

For Sanctification

Paul expands the writer of Hebrew's description of God's grand purpose for our suffering in his letter to the Romans,

> …we rejoice in our sufferings, knowing that suffering produces endurance, and endurance produces character, and character produces hope, and hope does not put us to shame because God's love has been poured into our hearts through the Holy Spirit who has been given to us.[120]

One of the most profound yet paradoxical statements in Scripture has to be: "we rejoice in our suffering." It is a preposterous notion that we could ever find joy in our suffering, but Paul teaches us just that. He teaches us suffering is the tool of God to conform us into the image of Christ. We rejoice in our suffering because we know it produces something greater. It is not our end, nor will it bring everlasting destruction to us; it is for our good we suffer.

---

119   Hebrews 12:11
120   Romans 5:3-5

Such a radical response to suffering as joy also displays the supreme worth of God. We are prone to grumble and become increasingly impatient with our earthly condition, and it isn't natural for us to rejoice in our suffering. So, when a Christian displays joy and patience in their suffering, they display to the world they have found something of great value, so great, in fact, their whole attitude towards suffering changes from negative to positive.

We must endure in our suffering, not only because we become more like Christ, but also because it glorifies God. Suffering transforms broken people into beautiful pieces of art, which is what Paul tells us when he writes, "For we are his workmanship, created in Christ Jesus for good works, which God prepared beforehand, that we should walk in them."[121] Suffering is for our good because it is God's tool for sanctification.

For Testing the Genuineness of Our Faith

To any sane person, it seems, joy and suffering are worlds apart, and no one can experience consistent joy in suffering. However, the Bible calls us to do it; and in the New Testament Jesus, Paul, Peter, and James clearly expect Christians to be joyful in their trials and suffering.

We have already seen two of God's purposes for our suffering and how they cause joy in us. Peter's illustration of the purification of gold[122] gives us a third reason for joy in suffering. The first two reasons we rejoice are because our impurities are removed through the intense heat. The third reason is assurance of genuine faith.

---

121   Ephesians 2:10
122   1 Peter 1:7

God gives us trials without regard to our good works, He gives according to what we can bear. This means the best and most assured Christians are just as likely possible recipients of suffering as those who lack in maturity and assurance.

For those who lack faith, trials facilitate the increase of faith by forcing them to understand the Scriptures better and grow in their trust for Christ. For those with great faith, trials reorient them with dependence on God alone. Wherever you and I land on that scale, trials are good for us because they are intended for our good. They don't exist for God to be assured of our faith, but to tangibly assure us of our faith in Christ.

When Christians enter a trial, especially a severe one, the great question on their minds is if and when they will know when the trial is over. In the moment of trial, it seems so overwhelming that there is no chance of overcoming or even recovering from it. What signifies the end of a trial? From my experience, it is a realization of complete peace with the existence of the trial and a clear observation of the growth produced by it. Thanksgiving from the heart for the trial is the best indication we've come through the valley of suffering. It is like hiking in the mountains. Halfway up the mountain, we are out of the valley, but it still takes difficult climbing to get to the breathtaking mountaintop view. Likewise, thanksgiving usually happens well after the trial is actually over.

We glorify God by joyful endurance, by knowing trials indicate the strength of our faith, by assuring us we are in Christ, and by pointing out weaknesses for us to target for growth. In every part of our trials, Paul's encouragement stands true: "We know that for those who love God all things work together for good."[123]

---

123   Romans 8:28

For a Display of Glory

The ultimate purpose of our trials is to display the glory of God. Jesus summarized the purpose of suffering when telling His disciples of His imminent death and the suffering they would face because of it:

> Truly, truly, I say to you, when you were young, you used to dress yourself and walk wherever you wanted, but when you are old, you will stretch out your hands, and another will dress you and carry you where you do not want to go. (This he said to show by what kind of death he was to glorify God.)[124]

Again, the Scripture plainly states that to suffer for the sake of Christ, in following Him and becoming more like Him, displays the glory of God. What do others see when a Christian suffers for the sake of Christ? They see one who has found a good master, one who will lose everything for His service. This risk is foreign to those under the rule of this world's master. Under his rule, their temporal desires are gratified enough to make them forget about eternity for a moment. But, he promises them what he cannot ultimately deliver. The good master of heaven, however, fills the believer with eternal joys and satisfaction, and so they do not seek the glory and pomp of earthly kings but suffer cheerfully for the sake of their King.

SUFFERING REPROACH

We have seen how it is common for love and hatred to walk hand in hand in the things for which we are most passionate.

---

124   John 21:18-19

Another aspect of passion is disdain for any negative comment or action directed at the object of passion. Negative comments and actions are taken personally. When people do this, they take upon themselves the reproach of what they love. So it is when we come to believe in God. Not only does the Holy Spirit cause us to believe in God, but He brings us along by the same means to love and adore God, making us willing to suffer the reproach of Him.

Since men naturally love darkness, Christians who dwell in the light are repugnant to them, and must by any means be dealt with. It should never come as a surprise to those in Christ when they are slandered, disgraced, and criticized for His sake. They must expect and embrace the unpleasant and oftentimes hurtful attacks because it glorifies God.

King David understood this well when he pleads with God to deliver him from the reproach he received from his 'friends' and enemies. He cried out,

> "For it is for your sake that I have borne reproach, that dishonour has covered my face. I have become a stranger to my brothers, an alien to my mother's sons. For zeal for your house has consumed me, and the reproaches of those who reproach you have fallen on me."[125]

Bearing scorn for the sake of another is evidence of a close bond. We see this in David's cry for help, "I have become a stranger to my brothers, an alien to my mother's sons." The honour of God caused even the closest of earthly relationships to be broken. For this to happen, the tie which bound David to God had to be more sure and steadfast than his familial bonds. David explains the extent of this dishonour:

---

125   Psalm 69:7-9

> When I wept and humbled my soul with fasting, it became
> my reproach. When I made sackcloth my clothing, I be-
> came a byword to them. I am the talk of those who sit in
> the gate, and the drunkards make songs about me. [126]

David was brought low by the people around him for the
sake of God. He was aware of the glory of God and the reproach
of man which followed, and the reproach he bore is the same we
bear today.

The reason we bear the reproach of God is because God
has bound us to Himself by adopting us as His children. When
Jesus taught His disciples to pray, "Our Father in heaven," He
was saying something no one had ever said before. No one, not
even the prophets of the Old Testament or the patriarchs, dared
to call God their Father in a personal sense. It was heretical in
the ears of the religious leaders, and they were ready to kill Jesus
because of it.[127] The charge made against one who called God
their Father was they made themselves a son of God. To claim
sonship was problematic because it was equivocal to claiming
equality with the Father, because in that time, a son was a sure
heir to *all* a father possessed.

Paul followed this teaching of Jesus by making the same
claim. In his letter to the Romans, Paul first established he was
the *doúlos* (bondservant) of Jesus Christ, but he goes on to say
he is a son of God and an heir with Christ: "The Spirit himself bears witness with our spirit that we are children of God,
and if children, then heirs—heirs of God and fellow heirs with
Christ."[128] How can it be a slave inherits what the son inherits?
To find the answer, we must look to the cross. Jesus Christ took
the place of the slave so the slave could have the status of the

---

126   Psalm 69:10-12
127   John 5:18
128   Romans 8:16-17a

son. As Jesus hung on the cross, God turned His back toward His Son, making Christ an orphan. Jesus Christ became an orphan so we, orphaned and alienated from God, could become children of God. Since we are now children of God, we are associated with God, and we bear the reproach against God. We say with David, "The reproaches of those who reproach you have fallen on me."

There is, what seems to be, a law in glorifying God that God enables us to glorify Him, and because of glorifying Him, He blesses us. Likewise, God enables us to honour Him, and in return, He honours us. So when we honour God and receive dishonour from the world, God is pleased to honour us. It is a similar law to what we find in salvation. God saves us by His grace alone and blesses us because of it. God's mercy and grace to us is truly mercy upon mercy and grace upon grace.

In this world, we take heart because Christ has overcome the world. Because Christ has overcome the world, our suffering ends up benefiting us. We feel pain in our suffering, but that pain is overcome through faith in the promises of God. Contentment floods our soul in the shadow of God's providence. Joy replaces bitterness and contempt for the existence of pain. So, spend time in God's promises and you will glorify Him through your suffering by your contentment, comfort, joy, and peace.

CHAPTER SIX

The Glory of God in Daily Life

EVERY ASPECT OF THE CHRISTIAN LIFE IS TOUCHED BY THE GLORY OF God, both in God working within the Christian and the Christian glorifying God as a result. This means the daily public and private activities of each Christian are meant to glorify God. Many incorrectly think this means consciously giving God glory in every step and action, but it's not that. It is, rather, the actions themselves glorify God when performed with the correct desire. To act in such a way, Christians must have a character predisposed to doing everything for God's glory. Spiritual growth plays an important part in becoming such a Christian, but the question, as this chapter looks to answer, is, what do Christians do to live their daily lives to the glory of God?

A CAUSE WORTH LIVING FOR

The essence of living for a cause is to change all aspects of life to commit fully to that cause. It is all or nothing. If other causes draw attention away from the initial cause, it proves that person was not living for the initial cause. This is precisely what Jesus teaches us in His Sermon on the Mount: "No one can serve two masters, for either he will hate the one and love the other, or he will be devoted to one and despise the other. You cannot serve God and money."[129]

There are only two religions in the world; the worship of God, and the worship of creation.[130] Jesus did not say it is impossible to have two masters, but that it is impossible to *serve* two masters. A master is one who rules over his subjects, and it is treason for a subject to devote their time and attention to the cares of another master, or to use our modern language, it is impossible for an employee to work two full-time jobs during the same hours. We are created to serve one master, and no technological advances to ease the load of two masters could ever help us properly serve them. Yet we try. We try to fit Scripture into the form of our lives; we try to serve both God and whatever this world offers. It is especially true for those of us who, for the most part, live comfortable lives. After taking care of essentials such as food, shelter, and clothing, we have some left over, and with the vast array of luxuries and accessories available, we tend to use that excess money to indulge ourselves. We may even take a step further and forgo some of the basic necessities to obtain more luxuries. Our lives are nice. The money we get and the things we can purchase with that money are nice. So, we accommodate Scripture to fit our lives by creating a nice Jesus according to our society's standard. We create a Jesus who has a similar mentality about money. This Jesus understands how necessary nice things are. He understands a bigger television, a nicer car, and a larger house are *essentials* for our survival. But this Jesus is not God.

When we read Jesus' conversation with the rich young ruler,[131] our response is much the same as the young ruler. Not only

---

129   Matthew 6:24
130   Romans 1:25
131   Luke 18:18-30

do we walk away dejected, but we also try to justify our wealth. We say, "But Jesus, don't you understand how things work in our culture? You can't be serious about giving it all away?" All we do is further prove we deserve the same command the young ruler received.

Does this mean we must hate money and pursue poverty? No. Does this mean we cannot be rich? Again, no. Jesus does not condemn wealthy people for being wealthy; He condemns them for loving their wealth. Our money is a resource that displays our hearts in a manner like none other. This means that if we go on spending like the rest of the world, buying for the same reasons they buy, perhaps buying many of the same luxuries they buy, we do not use our money in a way that shows we are living for God. I would agree with others who have said there is no teaching of Christ concerning money, which does not convict us. Our money shows us where our hearts truly are. It shows us whether we are serving God or ourselves.

The biblical picture of serving two masters is larger than wealth and possessions. There is a spiritual application, as well. In Paul's letter to the Philippians, Paul tells us the Law is another master contending against God for our service. He goes on to list his impressive religious resume to show what he is giving up for the sake of Christ, and if we were to convert his resume into money, he would be one of the wealthiest ever to live. His attitude towards Christ, however, was much different than the rich young ruler:

> "Whatever gain I had, I counted as loss for the sake of Christ. Indeed, I count everything as loss because of the surpassing worth of knowing Christ Jesus my Lord. For his

sake I have suffered the loss of all things and count them as
rubbish, so that I may gain Christ."[132]

To gain Christ, Paul had to count everything as loss. He
could not gain Christ unless he left behind all of his own efforts
and righteousness. From this, we find two realities: Christ's righteousness far surpasses the best righteousness of man, and man
cannot have Christ's righteousness without forsaking his own.

Likewise, Paul could not gain Christ if he desired money more than Christ. In his worldview, to know Christ and be
united to Him exceeded everything this world could offer. In
fact, all the pleasures and luxuries the world had to offer were
to him as useless as trash. Instead, he pursued contentment.[133]
He understood desiring wealth and loving money produced all
kinds of evils and destruction.[134] Like Christ's righteousness, not
only is Christ much greater than money, Christ cannot be served
at the same time as money.

Living for God must be complete, since God commands
every part of our being to love him. When we use our money,
our time, and whatever other resources we have for God, we
glorify Him. We display to the world that Christ is far greater than anything the world can offer; we display the surpassing
worth of knowing God through Christ. This means we cut all
ties with this world and the sin which remains. We glorify God
when we lay aside everything we once thought as being worthwhile to gain more of Christ.

Living for God means we spend our lives for Him; we
present ourselves fully at His service. We are ambassadors for
Christ in this world. We are aliens making a pilgrimage through

---

132   Philippians 3:7-8
133   Philippians 4:10-13
134   1 Timothy 6:6-10

a foreign land. We are merchants trading for the master's interest. We do not hide the fact we are from a different place.

A CHEERFUL LIFE

To glorify God, the Christian life ought to be a cheerful life. This might sound out of place in light of this chapter's focus on trials, tribulations, and persecution in the Christian life. How can someone maintain cheerfulness in such a fallen world? Of the many reasons I could give you, Paul gives us the greatest: the doctrine of justification by faith alone.

> Therefore, since we have been justified by faith, we have peace with God through our Lord Jesus Christ. Through him we have also obtained access by faith into this grace in which we stand, and we rejoice in hope of the glory of God.[135]

Doctrine is often considered by twenty-first-century Christians to be unnecessary and antiquated, but nothing could be further from the truth. Doctrine is simply a belief or set of beliefs—which everyone has to some extent. In many of Paul's letters, he sets doctrine as the foundation of the Christian life, and we learn from him out of doctrine flows all Christian living. So, when he declares our justification has produced peace with God, he is proclaiming joy-inducing news. We, who were enemies of God and destined for destruction, have received redemption; what more do we need for us to live joyous and cheerful lives?

The necessary cheerful disposition of the Christian *must flow from* the belief in the doctrine of justification by faith alone. All other forms of cheerfulness are unhelpful and false because

---

135   Romans 5:1-2

they are circumstantial, not eternal; there is no sure foundation to keep it from being washed to sea. When we have peace with God, we walk cheerfully with God.

As we walk with God, we are consumed by grace. Again, the result is cheerfulness. Paul puts it this way, "We rejoice in hope of the glory of God." Those who are justified, Paul says, exult or rejoice in the promise of future glory. John Calvin, when considering this phrase, commented: "Paul's meaning is, that though the faithful are now pilgrims on the earth, they yet by hope scale the heavens, so that they quietly enjoy in their own bosoms their future inheritance."[136] Because God declares us righteous in Christ, Calvin is saying, we possess a cheerful disposition as we walk this earth. We rest on the sure foundation of God's favour towards us, and the peace we gain from this new reality makes sweet music deep within us, even when great storms surround us. On that foundation we find joy, and with it, a cheerfulness that cannot be snuffed out by the world, the flesh, or the devil.

Paul continues in Romans 5 to argue this joy of a future hope causes us to have joy in our present sufferings.

> Not only that, but we rejoice in our sufferings, knowing that suffering produces endurance, and endurance produces character, and character produces hope, and hope does not put us to shame, because God's love has been poured into our hearts through the Holy Spirit who has been given to us.[137]

To bring Paul's argument into our day and age, and into our western culture, takes some doing because we haven't experienced persecution for our faith in tortures or martyrdom like

---

136   From Calvin's Commentary on Romans 5:2
137   Romans 5:3-5

those early Christians or the Christians in certain parts of the modern world. We do experience the curse of sin, but we have yet to face persecution for our faith. However, that doesn't mean we won't see it in our lifetimes. A lot of our perceived suffering is what some call "luxury suffering." We add this luxury suffering to the list of suffering from sin's curse, but it is not the same, and we shouldn't continue to consider it as such. Nevertheless, the curse which we experience in sickness, pain, relational problems, and death, along with persecution, are part of the sufferings to which Paul refers. Paul reiterates the last beatitude, which speaks of how those persecuted for Christ are *makarios*, which, though often translated "blessed," means fortunate, well-off, and happy. So, when Paul says we rejoice in suffering, he is, indeed, talking about a cheerful embrace of the suffering faced for the cause of Christ and for the cause of making us more like Christ.

This cheerfulness is not a giddy attitude, either. It is a natural cheerfulness flowing from a joy secured in the infinite foundation of eternal life. This eternal promise is where the cords of joy and cheerfulness intertwine. Cheerfulness is natural to the Christian because of the work which God has done in them.

Martyn Lloyd-Jones, a pastor in London during the Second World War and the following moral revolution, saw if Christians are not cheerful, they not only miss out on the benefits of the Christian life, they are defective Christians.

> Christians, as is obvious from the New Testament, are meant to be rejoicing people. They are partakers of the 'so great salvation' (Heb. 2:3). They are people, therefore, who should 'rejoice evermore' (1 Thess. 5:16). That is the terminology used in the New Testament itself and if we are not in that condition, if we are not giving the impression to the world that we are in this happy position, then we are

very defective as Christians and we are missing so much that God offers to us freely through his dear Son, our Lord and Saviour.[138]

We must, then, be cheerful as we walk this pilgrim way. By our cheerfulness, we glorify God because we display to the world we've found an anchor for our soul. We tell others by our attitude our master is kind and gentle, and has promised a great inheritance for us. We display the satisfaction and peace our adoption into the family of God gives our longing hearts. When we live like this, we "serve the Lord with gladness."[139] According to Thomas Watson, the Christian's disposition of cheerfulness is the result of true religion: "[True] religion does not take away our joy, but refines it; it does not break our violin, but tunes it, and makes the music sweeter."[140]

VOCATION AND DAILY LIFE

If you are even slightly familiar with the sixteenth-century Reformation, you are aware of the important part doctrine and biblical theology played in reforming the Church. What is not as well-known is how the Reformation changed the way people lived their practical day-to-day lives. Particularly, the idea of vocation (or calling) was uncovered alongside the gospel. Vocation, according to the Church at that time, was God's special calling to live a life glorifying Him, which they understood only pertained to the priesthood or monastic life. The Reformer's rescue of the gospel from Rome's control awakened the common people to understand their ordinary occupations were callings

---

138   Martyn Lloyd-Jones, *Born of God: Sermons from John 1* [Carlisle, PA: Banner of Truth Trust, 2011], 18.

139   Psalms 100:2

140   Thomas Watson, *A Body of Divinity* (Carlisle, PA: Banner of Truth Trust, 2015), 13.

as well. They saw the work which they did to make a living as a means by which they could glorify God. Not only that, but every mundane, common, and menial task was for the glory of God too.

The Reformed understanding of vocation is needed today as our current post-modern culture is most concerned with working for the benefit of self, not the glory of God, causing us to return to the pre-Reformation dark ages of despair and anxiety. The remedy is to look outside ourselves, to live for something greater than us. And what is greater than the glory of God?

What does it mean for Christians to glorify God in the ordinary tasks of life? It means we have an eye toward God in all we do. It means the greatness and majesty of God are the leading factors determining what we do and how we do it, and this attitude affects us from eating and drinking to buying and selling. To prove this point to a greater extent, glorifying God in the daily tasks of life is so important Paul took the time to remind two different churches of it. To the Colossians he wrote: "And whatever you do, in word or deed, do everything in the name of the Lord Jesus, giving thanks to God the Father through him."[141] And to the Corinthians he said " So whether you eat or drink, or whatever you do, do all to the glory of God."[142]

In eating and drinking, God gives us food for His service, so to glorify Him, food and drink must not fuel our lusts, but rather fuel obedience. Our eating and our drinking remind us our lives are not our own. We are bought with the price of Christ so we can live for God, and the sustenance we get from food and drink carry us on in our earthly service. We respond in

---

141   Colossians 3:17
142   1 Corinthians 10:31

thankfulness because it reorients us to the giver and the purpose of what is given.

In buying and selling, we display the glory of God by properly conducting our business. There are unbelievers who display the glory of God in their business without intending to, but many who do not have an eye toward God seek unjust gain by falsifying balances, charging more than what the product or service is worth, or they purposely fail to report certain financial gain. The load of their financial stress may be lifted for a time, but the weight of sin only increases. To "do unto others as you would have them do to you" is the way we glorify God in our daily transactions. No conscious person desires to be taken advantage of, stolen from, or cheated. So, too, we must act in our business that we do not offend one another by it. The underlying principle of glorifying God in buying and selling is to do so in kindness and honesty.

Glorifying God in the small things is the measuring stick of glorifying Him in the big things. When we think of glorifying God, we usually think of the grand things such as salvation or praising His character, actions, and attributes. In practical living, we think the grand things are going far away for mission work, seeing a massive response to evangelism, or anything else outstanding enough for people to notice. While the grand things are certainly glorious, we tend to forget the common and less impressive things in life are also glorious. We fall into the trouble of loving big moments and extraordinary things. The trouble with loving those moments and chasing after them is that as time goes on, our expectation for big moments and extraordinary things tends to expand so that the events must be bigger and more extraordinary to meet our expectations. If we fall prey to our expectations, we will find it difficult to praise and glorify God for the grand things, let alone the small things. It is perfectly good for us to glorify God in His grandeur and good-ness, but it is equally good for us to glorify Him in the seemingly insignificant things. In fact, if we do not glorify Him in insig-nificant things, we *cannot* glorify Him in the grand things. Why is this so? It is because the glory of God is a whole glory; there is no separation of small and great, or significant and insignifi-cant. Since all things made by God are for God,[143] we cannot be pickers and choosers about the things in which we glorify God.

Glorifying God in both our vocation and daily life is not naturally or immediately brought about. Instead, we grow into it. Our growth in holiness, a process of separation from self-glo-rification towards the glory of God, is the end to which we have been saved. Paul's instructions to the Thessalonians instruct us in this matter:

> We urge you, brothers, admonish the idle, encourage the fainthearted, help the weak, be patient with them all. See that no one repays anyone evil for evil, but always seek to do good to one another and to everyone. Rejoice always, pray without ceasing, give thanks in all circumstances; for this is the will of God in Christ Jesus for you.[144]

It is the will of God for us to do these things, and if it is God's will, it is for His glory. God is concerned with our daily tasks and run-of-the-mill events because they display just how deep God's involvement is in our lives and the extent to which the work of God in Christ goes to change us. God's work in us happens when we renew our minds each day in the truth of the grandest glory, the gospel.[145] By renewing our minds in

---

143   Romans 11:36
144   1 Thessalonians 5:14-18
145   Romans 12:1-2

God's Word, we will not conform to the pattern of this world, which glorifies man, but we will be transformed into the image of Christ who glorified God perfectly. The gospel changes our outlook from a man-centred perspective into a Christ-centred perspective which, without a doubt, changes the way we conduct ourselves in every aspect of life.

CONCLUSION

Enjoying God

IN A SENSE, THE QUESTION, "HOW CAN WE GLORIFY GOD?" IS similarly expressed in the question, "How can we enjoy God?" Each practical way Christians glorify God greatly enhances their ability to enjoy God. When Christians praise God for salvation, work diligently to rid themselves of sin, publicly display their faith, suffer for God's sake, and live every part and parcel of their lives to the glory of God, they live the most satisfying and enjoyable way possible, just as the Creator intended. Sin robbed humanity of every satisfaction, and unless God saves, no one reclaims that satisfaction regardless of how hard they try. We find this in Solomon's attempt to satisfy every desire by earthly things. What did he get out of it? Nothing. Meaninglessness. By the time he had wasted a good portion of his resources on finding enjoyment, he had learned a valuable lesson. "The end of the matter; all has been heard. Fear God and keep his commandments, for this is the whole duty of man."[146] In other words, Solomon concluded his search for enjoyment and satisfaction with only one option left: glorify God.

However, there is a sense in which the Westminster Divines meant something more in enjoying God than simply receiving enjoyment from glorifying God, and Thomas Watson picked up on it. According to Watson, enjoying God is found in communion with God. Enjoyment is more than the practical effects of glorifying Him; it is relating to Him as our loving Father. Therefore, at the end of answering the question of how we glorify God, we must answer this question: What does it look like to enjoy God?

The heart of the gospel is the promise of rest in Christ. This is the famous conviction of Augustine, "Our hearts are restless until they find their rest in thee." In Christ, we rest from sin and the Law, which covers ever endeavour of man. Sin is a treadmill where greedily lusting after power, status, possessions, and so on never quenches our deepest thirst. The Law is the suppressor, weighing each person down with guilt and fear of condemnation. All is toil because of sin and the moral law, but Christ was obedient in our place, and He became sin for us that we might find rest.

When we rest in Christ, not only do we find freedom from sin and the moral law, we find the enjoyment of God. In Christ, every attribute of God is for our good, whereas outside of Christ, every attribute of God is for our destruction. This is not to say Christ persuades God to be kind to us, but God's holiness and justice require payment for sin. Our dealings with God must first be judicial (at the cross) before they can be relational (in our hearts), and when they are relational, we experience God Himself. Thomas Watson declared God "is the *summum bonum*, the chief good." And when we enjoy Him, "the enjoyment of Him is the highest felicity." Watson's reasoning is this: if we know what kind of good God is, we know what kind of good we enjoy; and according to Watson, the kind of good God is, as found in the Bible, is an unmixed, satisfying, delicious, superlative, and eternal good.[147] In other words, God is the truest good who gives us the truest enjoyment.

The Divines didn't intend to communicate enjoyment in this present life only, but to extend the Christian's enjoyment of God into the depths of eternity. Watson describes what this enjoyment will be like, that it "will be in the perfection of holiness, in seeing the pure face of Christ, in feeling the love of God, in conversing with heavenly spirits; which will be proper for the soul, and infinitely exceed all carnal voluptuous delights."[148] Communion with God enjoyed here in this life continues seamlessly into the next life, albeit perfectly then.

The apostle Paul connects our future joy with our present joy, showing us there is not only a connection from our present enjoyment to our future enjoyment, but also from our future enjoyment to the present. "Through him we have also obtained access by faith into this grace in which we stand, *and we rejoice in hope of the glory of God*."[149] We rejoice now in the hope of a certain future. Paul understood the basic human need for joy in this life, and he understood the purest form of it is found only in the gospel promise of future enjoyment. Joy is positive hope, it is the essence of faith, and it glorifies God.

What is the meaning and purpose of life? It is to glorify God and enjoy Him forever. Meaningful purpose, then, only comes when we live our lives completely and functionally for God's glory, and in the joy communion with Him brings.

---

147   Thomas Watson, *A Body of Divinity* (Carlisle, PA: Banner of Truth Trust, 2015), 23.
148   Ibid., 24.
149   Romans 5:2 emphasis added.

Scripture
Index

Also by Daniel Klassen
Thinking Christianity

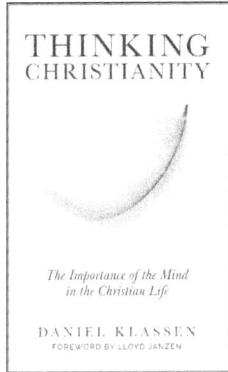

Christianity today faces a crisis in thinking: there is both an in-difference toward, and neglect of, serious thought about Christian doctrine and theology. Instead, personal experience has been given primacy. *Thinking Christianity* attempts to reverse this popular attitude and forestall the rejection of the Christian gospel that will otherwise inevitably follow.

Author Daniel Klassen covers two aspects of thinking in the Christian faith: the necessity for thinking, and the need for *proper* thinking. Throughout the book, he attempts to explore these with clarity and truthfulness by expounding Scripture, using historical examples from the Reformation, and exploring philosophical ideas. This clearly reasoned, timely book will help Christians live in assurance and confidence in God—and pre-serve the gospel for future generations.

ISBN
Paperback: 978-1-5255-3234-4
Hardcover: 978-1-5255-3233-7

www.ingramcontent.com/pod-product-compliance
Lightning Source LLC
LaVergne TN
LVHW051423080426
835508LV00022B/3216